MW01491165

Ordinary People:
Extraordinary Lessons

Ordinary People: Extraordinary Lessons

Leadership Insights from Everyday Encounters

KAREN FRIEDMAN
CEO, Karen Friedman Enterprises, Inc.
Author, *Shut Up and Say Something*

© 2017 Karen Friedman
All rights reserved.

ISBN: 1542591813
ISBN 13: 9781542591812
Library of Congress Control Number: 2017900757
CreateSpace Independent Publishing Platform
North Charleston, South Carolina

Foreword

Karen Friedman has always had a distinctive style. I remember her as a hard-hitting TV news reporter, and the same attention to detail and ability to pick up on the nuances of human experience are showcased in her essays.

The human perspective, exemplified in her anecdotes of everyday life, makes what she says relatable. Her words are never academic-sounding abstractions; they tell real stories about real people. You *know* the people she writes about. You've encountered them too. They're your customers, your friends, people you run across randomly, maybe even your annoying relatives; whomever they are, you *know* them.

That's what makes Karen's perspective so valuable. Her voice is the common-sense voice, the voice that speaks to us in language we understand but sometimes forget to listen to.

So pour yourself a cup of coffee, get comfortable on the couch, and delve into Karen's world. You'll find yourself learning something about people…and probably yourself.

Dell Poncet, managing editor, *Philadelphia Business Journal*

Celebrating twenty years in business and everyday encounters with so many valued clients and readers who have taught me extraordinary lessons.

Contents

Foreword · v
Introduction · xi

One   Customer Service· 1
Two   When Business Gets Personal · · · · · · · · · · · · · · · · 23
Three   Value Your Values · 43
Four   Performance · 64
Five   Sending the Wrong Message · · · · · · · · · · · · · · · · 88
Six   Proceed with Caution · 109
Seven   Love and Loyalty· 129

         About the Author · 147

Introduction

I started writing my column for the *Philadelphia Business Journal* to promote my book *Shut Up and Say Something*. Never did I imagine that what started as a marketing tactic would become a cherished pastime. And never did I imagine that, unlike my early articles, these columns would blossom into so much more and that I would bloom simply by learning from the people who grace their pages.

I never know what I'm going to write about because I never know what I'm going to see or experience from moment to moment. So I keep a notebook, and when I see something sad, funny, infuriating, out of the ordinary, or simply very ordinary, I jot it down. I may not know what message should be conveyed, but I know there is one.

The toughest part of writing this book has been figuring out which columns to choose. I've become attached to all of them. To me, each one has a message that's as important as the people who inspired them. Since it would be a bit lengthy to reprint seven years of columns, I've chosen those with the most teachable moments. These are encounters that happen anywhere—in a supermarket, in an office, or while walking the dog.

It's these little everyday moments we all experience that can often teach the biggest lessons—that is, if we keep our eyes, ears, and hearts open wide enough to recognize their meaning.

Karen

One

Customer Service

Welcome To Philadelphia

Welcome to Philadelphia. Or maybe not. Arriving at the Thirtieth Street station to catch the Amtrak to Washington, DC, should be a welcoming experience, especially if you're visiting from out of town. Fortunately, I'm a resident and have come to expect a certain amount of rude behavior from Philadelphians assigned to help.

Wondering what track my train typically arrives on, I inquired at the information desk.

"The train isn't posted yet," she said.

"I know," I responded. "I was just wondering what track it usually arrives on."

"Ma'am…we have late trains to deal with that take priority, so if your train is not late, you'll just have to wait."

"My train isn't late," I said, pointing to the big information board above her head. "It's the 8:17 a.m. that says, 'On time to DC.' I just want to know what track it's expected to arrive on so I can sit by that track."

"Ma'am, I told you we are quite busy with late trains."

I looked up at the board again, and in the status column, every train read "on time."

"Well," I remarked, "I was just asking a question."

"Which," she hissed, "I answered.

So I sat down and looked around at the early-morning travelers, many of whom were standing, looking up at the information board, and clearly trying to determine where to catch their trains.

That's when I did a quick poll asking people where they were from. Boston. Baltimore. Pittsburgh. Rhode Island.

"Excuse me," said a Boston-bound passenger to me. "Do you happen to know what track the train to DC is on?"

Thinking better of sending her to the information desk, I said, "I didn't, but eventually it will be posted on the board."

I've written about this before. Taxi drivers, information desks, tour guides, street workers, or park rangers are our visitors' first impressions of Philadelphia. If you're not up to a warm smile, helpful hand, and friendly approach, perhaps you should do the city and public relations effort a favor and find a job without public interaction.

As I looked around, I noticed people starting to line up at track five. The Boston passenger was in line too. Assuming it was my train heading for DC, I got in line behind her.

"Excuse me, I'm sorry to bother you again," said Boston, "but do you know if this is the line for the train to DC? I asked the lady at the desk, and she said it was late, so it didn't have a track yet."

I glanced up at the board. Train #2107 to DC was still on time, leaving on track five.

"Yes, you're in the right line," I said, pointing to the board. Then I had an idea. I asked Boston to hold my place for a moment and walked back up to the information desk.

"Excuse me," I said. "Does train 2107 to DC have a track yet?"

"I told you it was late," she said, without looking up to meet my eye.

"Well, it's not late," I said, pointing to the board. "The board behind you says it's on time at track five, so perhaps you should look at it so you can help people."

She looked up, this time silently staring at me. Then she said, "Next."

"Next?" I asked. "What does 'next' mean?"

"I'll take the next person in line," she said.

So I stepped aside. Welcome to Philadelphia.

What's In A Title?
Watch Out For Those Chief Jargon Officers

Whenever I call my bank, no one calls me back. Since the phones apparently do not ring aloud, I have driven to the bank and spoken to the manager in person. He profusely apologizes and promises it won't happen again. Then, of course, it does.

The latest round of unreturned calls and voice mails to inquire about unrecognized charges on a statement began two weeks ago, but it wasn't until today that I got through to someone on the phone. Admittedly, I was angry and let him know it. He reacted by saying, "I've called you back repeatedly."

Like a counterpunch at a presidential debate, I said, "That is simply not true, and you know it. My caller ID and voice mail are working." Silence.

Finally, he said, "Ms. Friedman, I apologize for the inconvenience, but as the customer relationship manager, I'm here to help you." I almost fell off my chair. Customer relationship manager? Was this a joke? We have no relationship, and he clearly wasn't doing much to manage this one. Do organizations really think titles will be so impressive that they'll influence our way of thinking?

Titles used to be simple and easy to understand. Doctor. Lawyer. Journalist. Sales manager. Waiter. Today, many seem more creative and attention grabbing. They cleverly focus on outcomes or offer employees a more impressive way to define their roles. When CareerBuilder asked readers to share their unusual job titles, they heard from a "chief wiggle eye gluer," a "director of chaos," and a "head worm wrangler." I'm not sure what all of those people actually do for a living, but the "marble lady" who wrote in said she gives presentations about marbles. I got that.

The issue as I see it is that people want to stand out. I'm guilty too. Though my official title is president of Karen Friedman Enterprises, my business cards say "Chief Improvement Officer" because that's really what we do—we help people improve the way they communicate. Clever? Perhaps. More memorable than *president*? Absolutely.

The problem occurs when people craft titles that are not synonymous with what they do. Let's go back to the bank associate. He doesn't really manage customer relationships. He defends his actions, so a more suitable title for him might be "bank fee defender." Human resource professionals have become "talent development managers," and janitors have become "sanitation engineers." Then there is the ambiguous title of "solutions manager." What solutions are you providing, and how are you different from the company down the street? Aren't most companies in business to provide solutions?

> The problem occurs when people craft titles that are not synonymous with what they do

There are the longer, complicated titles like "refinery processing control accounting manager" or "associate director of strategic forecasting for antibacterial and antifungal diseases." These titles allow you to appear smart, impressive, and important even though most people have no clue what you do for a living. I wonder if titles reflect the way a person communicates.

While on the phone trying to change an airline ticket, the "reservation and transportation ticket agent" asked me what "revenue stream" I wanted to pay with. "Excuse me?" I asked She was referring to the credit card I wanted to use.

This brings me back once again to my bank's customer relationship manager. As we tried to get to the bottom of the fee issue, he explained that my previous account wasn't "categorized as a performance account with secondary formal protection" and assured me he would "reach out to his business segmentation team and have them tag the accounts appropriately." Sure, whatever you say.

As I was writing this column, my dad called. He and my mom, who volunteer at a South Florida hospital, said the gobble-de-gook has spilled over into office hallways as well. Dad complained that people can no longer find the self-explanatory Office of Medical Records, which had been changed to HIM, which stands for Health Information Management. Only the new sign didn't clearly explain that these departments were one and the same. My dad joked with visitors: "If they couldn't find HIM, they should look for HER, which he dubbed "help eliminate rhetoric."

Personally, I'm exhausted trying to decipher all this grandiose language on a regular basis. And, by the way, the phone just rang. To my surprise, it was my banking relationship manager. He said he was trying to get to the bottom of my problem, but he didn't understand what I meant by "unrecognized charges."

As my teenage son would say, "My bad."

I'll try to be clearer next time.

Lessons Learned From A Vendor/Customer E-Mail War

I don't take pleasure in firing vendors or anyone, for that matter, though this may be the exception. "Michael," as I'll call him, had handled our payroll for years. Every year, I watched our fees go up with no notice or explanation, so this year, I inquired as to why his rates were outpacing inflation.

I was told it's because he has the "best payroll staff in the industry," and therefore, he increases their pay each year. He went on to say that he was competitive and customers who have left him often came back because other firms "typically screwed things up." Annoyed, I dashed off a terse e-mail to our CFO saying, "That's the kind of thing people say when they don't have a real reason." Then I hit Send just a bit too quickly. I accidentally sent the e-mail to Michael.

Instead of picking up the phone and calling me to better understand why a long-time client was upset or taking a moment to wonder how other clients may react, he immediately responded with an e-mail that said, "Please find a new payroll company."

Slightly embarrassed, I picked up the phone and called him. No response. I e-mailed an apology. No answer. Our CFO tried to patch things up. No luck. I realized there are numerous teachable moments from this incident that can be applied in a wide variety of situations.

TEACHABLE MOMENT #1: NO KNEE JERKING
If you've served a customer for a long time, instead of instantly reacting, take a pause and then initiate a conversation to better understand why the customer is upset. You might quickly repair

the problem and use what you learn to improve relationships with other customers.

Given that didn't happen, we found a new payroll partner. Yet weeks later, I received Michael's monthly electronic newsletter. I scrolled to the bottom and opted out only to receive another e-mail from him saying he needed more specifics so he would know what e-mails I didn't want to receive. Annoyed again, I responded that I didn't want any correspondence from him at all.

Imagine my surprise when I received a mass e-mail weeks later after I had forgotten about the incident. This one invited those on his list to visit a booth he'd rented at a trade show. At the end of the e-mail, it said, "This e-mail was sent to a long list of folks in my contact list. If it doesn't apply to you, please ignore."

TEACHABLE MOMENT #2: UPDATE YOUR SUBSCRIBER LIST
It's important to go through your subscriber list on a regular basis to make sure you respect those who don't want to hear from you. Additionally, electronic marketing is not about mass e-mails. Rather, it's about segmenting your list so you send the right e-mails to the right people.

So I opted out again, only to receive another e-mail from him. This one, laced with sarcasm, said, "With pleasure. Best of luck in your 'public relations' business."

TEACHABLE MOMENT #3: STOP THE CONVERSATION
I knew better than to keep the conversation going. I knew that I should simply mark Michael's e-mails as spam. I knew nothing good could come if I responded, but I just couldn't help myself. My e-mail back to him said, "I'm not in public relations."

We're communication coaches, which is sometimes confused with public relations, but it's a nit and unimportant. I was purposely needling him, suggesting he should better understand what his clients do for a living.

He e-mailed me back. "Whatever you do, it shouldn't have anything to do with people."

Teachable Moment #4: Don't Make It Personal

Clearly ignoring what I teach, I did the opposite and spit an angry e-mail back. This one suggested he start thinking about his customers instead of himself before he sends obnoxious e-mails. I asked him never to contact me again.

But since I was to blame for violating teachable moment #3, he immediately retorted that I had the market cornered on obnoxious e-mails and that he's been very successful for many years and has no intention of changing the way he does things.

Teachable Moment #5: Get Over Yourself

Learning is or should be a lifelong process. That means learning from our mistakes and trying to see things from someone else's perspective. But if you think that your way is the only way, you'll react defensively instead of recognizing potential opportunities.

I came across a quote recently that said, "Life is 10% what happens to you and 90% how you react to it." We all react poorly at times. Even though the customer isn't always right, as a vendor, you work for them. When you take a moment to acknowledge and understand their concerns, you become more customer focused instead of me focused, which is the best public relations.

Coupon Cops:
How Employees Can Tarnish Your Reputation

I walked into a high-end women's store that was having a 30 percent–off sale. In addition to the already slashed prices, I had an additional 15 percent–off coupon that said, "Extra savings; use any time." The fine print specified no restrictions whatsoever. Good deal!

So I chose a dress. When I went to pay for it, I gave the saleswoman my coupon, which she said didn't apply. "Why?" I inquired She informed me that coupons didn't apply to sale items. I pointed out what my coupon said, which led to a thorough examination of it on her part. Tick tock. "Is there a problem?" I asked.

"Well," she said without any explanation, "the coupon can't be used." I asked for a manager. The manager scoured the fine print of my questionable coupon and pronounced it valid. The clerk, who at this point I thought owned the store or had significant stock options, questioned the manager's opinion. So I chimed in, suggesting that they scan the coupon to see if it would work. It did, taking 15 percent off my already discounted purchase. The manager left. I pulled out my credit card to pay.

I could not have scripted what happened next. The clerk opened a drawer and pulled out a magnifying glass. "Excuse me," I said. "What are you doing?"

"Well," she said, "I'm sure there is a reason you are not allowed to use this coupon." I looked for an armband designating her a coupon cop but couldn't find one.

"Listen," I said, "can I just pay?" That's when another salesperson came over and started discussing lunch break plans while I continued to stand there. Tick tock. Really? "Excuse me," I said again. "I'd like to pay for my purchase."

"Just a second," said the coupon cop. "I'll be right with you."

This is a major retailer. According to Market Pulse, its third-quarter profit last year was over forty-one million dollars. I don't get it. Clearly, they spend money on training. Clearly, they understand the value of customer service. And clearly, an additional 15 percent savings to a customer will not affect their bottom line in a big way.

I could post my experience on Facebook. I could tweet it on Twitter. I could put a video on YouTube, or I could share my experience with my groups and connections on LinkedIn. If I did, imagine how many people could be turned off and shop elsewhere. Imagine how that could translate to far more than 15 percent.

Some people think that social media affects other people, that it doesn't apply to their industry. Wrong. Social media is like the old-fashioned telephone. You call Mary. She calls Sue. Sue calls Sam, and Sam calls Tom. Before you know it, one hundred people are bad-mouthing the retailer. Only today, it happens faster. In seconds, thousands or more can hear about some else's negative experience and spread the virtual word across the globe.

Regardless of where you work, when you speak to your company's customer, you become the face of your company. As that spokesperson, it is your job to represent your organization respectably.

You may think you are only interacting with one person, but in reality, you may be interacting with thousands who ultimately can affect your company's bottom line. All it takes is one person to start a cyber-conversation that tarnishes your reputation.

All for a coupon?

Your Call Is Very Important To Us

The Amtrak train from New York's Penn Station to Thirtieth Street in Philadelphia burped and lurched and suddenly screeched to a stop in Newark, New Jersey. As passengers wondered what happened, the conductor instructed everyone headed to Philadelphia to get off. He said the train had mechanical problems, and we were to wait on the platform for the next train to Philadelphia.

Given it was evening rush hour, when the next train arrived, it was packed, without a seat to be found. So, like others, I stood for the next one and a half hours. Only I was wearing high heels that quickly became uncomfortable. I was sandwiched in between two bouncy rail cars, standing shoulder to shoulder with two male strangers whose 24-hour deodorant was apparently on its twenty-fifth hour on this muggy summer evening. So, a little unsteady on my feet and staring to feel queasy, I held on, hoping for the best.

I get it. Things happen. If not having a seat on a train is the worst that happens, I'm pretty lucky. But given that I'd paid for a seat I never sat in, I thought it was only right that I request a refund. So, when back on steady ground, I called the 1-800 number I found at the bottom of Amtrak's website. After punching in numerous prompts, the recording informed me that I had a five-minute wait, but my call was very important to them. So I waited. And waited. And eventually, thirty-three minutes and thirty-four seconds later, I hung up.

Then I went back to the website to find the Contact Us button and hit Send to request a refund. A few days later, Amtrak apologized and said they were disappointed there were not enough seats for everyone. Then they said they couldn't provide a refund but would offer a transportation certificate that was good for one year and that my "patronage" was very important to them.

Only there was a catch. To redeem the certificate, I had to call Amtrak's Customer Relations department. Here we go again. Ten minutes, twenty minutes, forty minutes…I was still on hold. Every now and again, a recorded voice would assure me that my call was very important. Fifty-eight minutes and some seconds later, a real person finally picked up the phone and quickly issued my transportation credit.

But there was another catch. When I wanted to book my next ticket, I had to call back yet again for an agent to book the ticket and apply the credit. So I did, holding on once more until my so-called important call was answered and the issue was finally resolved.

> ## It seems as if no one really wants to talk to anyone voice to voice

In today's time-challenged business environment, it seems as if no one really wants to talk voice to voice anymore. It's quicker to dash off an e-mail, leave a voice mail, or submit a form than have a real, time-consuming conversation. However, if you or your business promises people their call or inquiry is important, make sure your actions match your words. If not, what you're really saying is that their call is not that important at all. If it were, they would have already been connected to someone who could help them.

For example, if the wait time is more than five minutes, offer alternative options for the best time for them to call you back or for you to call them. Make sure to follow through.

The same can be said for that exasperating phone call to a credit card company or bank. After spending five minutes punching in your card number, expiration date, and other numeric necessities, when a real person picks up the phone, he or she asks you to repeat everything you've just entered into their system. So what's the point of entering all that information in the first place?

Then there are those automated voices that promise to direct you to the right department if you answer just a few simple questions. Only, like the iPhone's electronic assistant, Siri, the voice recognition application doesn't always understand what you said, asking you to repeat yourself two or three times, and when you finally become exasperated and keep pounding zero to speak to a human, the system frequently directs you to the wrong department.

While technology can improve efficiency, it can also minimize personal interaction. It can make us doubt the sincerity of companies and brands if their customer service departments and support systems appear insincere.

The fix is simple. Say what you mean and mean what you say. If you don't mean it, then don't say it.

When A Hotel Is Driving You Crazy

I had stayed at the upscale hotel many times before, so I knew what to expect, which is why I kept returning. Yet on this beautiful, warm May evening, as I went to check in, the front desk computer froze. The clerk apologized. "Oh well," I said. "It happens, no big deal."

Twenty minutes later, the computer was still frozen and I was still standing, bags in hand, not checked in. As an apology, the front desk clerk offered an upgraded room, complimentary Internet service, and breakfast on the house. Very nice and much appreciated, but I couldn't take advantage of his generosity without a room. Tick tock. Another ten minutes passed. I was still waiting.

So I asked for a manager and inquired if he could put me in a room and retrieve my information later. "Sure," he said. As an apology for my inconvenience, he said he'd like to send up a complimentary bottle of wine. Great!

Finally, down the hall and up the elevator I went. But when I entered my upgraded room, it was warm and kind of stuffy. The temperature panel read eighty-one degrees. So I walked over to the control panel and started hitting the down arrow to lower the temperature. Nothing. I kept hitting the arrows. Still nothing. As someone who'd never excelled at engineering, I figured I was the problem and called the front desk. The clerk apologized and said he'd send someone right up, but no one came. So I called again.

Moments later, knock knock. The front desk clerk was at my door. Now that I was on a first-name basis with Dave, he wanted to come in and personally adjust the air conditioning so I'd be comfortable. I let him in. He fidgeted with the same controls I struggled with and announced that he couldn't figure it out either.

Knock knock. Now who was here? It was the man from engineering. He looked at the panel on the wall and explained that it wasn't working because the hotel hadn't switched over from heat to air conditioning yet.

"Do you mean to tell me the heat is on in this room?" I asked.

"Yes, ma'am."

I then asked if the hotel realized it is the month of May. He said they knew because other guests had been complaining but explained that it wasn't that simple to switch all the rooms from heat to air. He then went on to elaborate on the mechanics of the complicated process when I cut him off. The front desk clerk apologized and asked me if I'd like to move to another room. I asked if there would be air conditioning in the next room, which, obviously, there was not. He apologized again and asked if there was anything they could do for me. I suggested turning on the air. "It's very complicated," the engineer said again, and I asked them to please leave my room when there was yet another knock at the door. Now what?

Like a bad sitcom that wouldn't end, the manager entered carrying a giant fan, which he ordered the engineer to set up in the middle of my room and suggested that I turn it on and open the windows to circulate the air. My upgraded room overlooked I-95. Thanks, but no thanks. Finally, they left, dragging the fan with them.

Moments later, the phone rang. It was the desk clerk. He called to let me know that the hotel management had decided to turn the heat off and switch over to air conditioning, which should happen shortly. That's great news I say and thank him for calling.

As I started to settle in, the air began to purr. Things were looking up. But somewhere along the way, as the desk clerk and engineer had fiddled with the temperature box to try to cool the room, they must have turned it down so dramatically that, when the air conditioner finally kicked in, it did so with a vengeance.

The hot, stuffy room quickly turned cold, too cold. I put on a jacket and looked at the controls myself. The temperature now read fifty-eight degrees. Trying to warm up the room, I pressed the up arrow. Nothing. I pressed it again…and again. Still nothing. So I stood there, trying to figure out what to do next, when there was yet another knock at my door.

Dave was back. This time, he was carrying a platter of fresh fruit and chutney, which he set on the table while offering another apology for the inconvenience. Apology accepted. He commented that it was rather chilly in the room. I started to ask him if someone could figure out how to turn the air up so the room wouldn't be so cold and then thought better of it.

Fortunately, there was an extra blanket in the closet.

A Study In Contrast About How To Deal With Your Customers

Talk about a study in contrast.

Over the summer, a group of eight friends went to dinner at a well-known, rather high-end restaurant at the Jersey shore. We had a great big round table overlooking the ocean. The menu looked as great as the view. That's where our experience ended. Twenty minutes after we were seated, no one had come to take even a beverage order. After we flagged down the maître d, a waiter finally came, and then it was another twenty minutes before drinks were served. Okay, it happens.

But what happened next was a lesson in how to anger patrons and lose customers. When dinner was served, three of the entrees were not what people had ordered. One entrée was missing entirely, and yet another was not fully cooked. When we complained, there was no apology, just a murmured, "What do you want me to do?" from the waiter, so we called for the manager.

A few minutes later, the mishap was shared with him. Again, no apology, just a terse, "So if I give you a couple of drinks, will that make you happy?" And if you can't imagine an evening going from worse to even worse, then you should have been with us when the manager began blaming us, interrupting as we tried to explain what had happened and making excuses until we paid for what we ate and walked out.

Maybe they didn't care, but they should have. The experience was posted on Facebook. Complaints were phoned into corporate headquarters. Not only did they lose our business, but if all eight of us repeated the story, and those people repeated the story, and more people posted on social media, well, you get the idea. That could amount to a lot of lost customers and potential customers.

In fairness to this restaurant, a corporate spokesperson did call, and he sent a fifty-dollar gift certificate to be used by all eight of us the next time we wanted to dine there. If you're not quick at math, that's $6.25 per person, which can't even buy you a beverage. And why would we want to go there again?

Let's contrast this lack of customer service to another recent experience. Planning for a home full of company recently, I purchased three bunches of beautiful flowers at Trader Joes, which is a great store with exceptional customer service. Less than 24 hours later, the flowers were dead. Again, it happens.

Unfortunately, this was the second time it had happened to me, so I filled out a form on the website letting them know. I wasn't mad, didn't want anything in return, and just suggested perhaps something was going on at this store that needed correcting.

Minutes after I hit Send, the manager from my local store called and profusely apologized. He said it was unacceptable and not only would he like to refund my flower money but, the next time I entertained at home, he wanted to pay for the entire meal. Wow! I was so startled by this over-the-top customer service that I was speechless. And because I was so appreciative that he called, I turned him down.

I would like to believe most people are not looking for a handout. Sure, there are some who will take advantage. But most of us simply want to know that those we deal with are customer focused and genuinely care about providing a great experience that makes us want to come back for more.

We don't want excuses. We want to know what you can do, not what you can't do. And if we're explaining a problem to you, we don't want you to keep jumping in because that means you don't care enough to listen.

No matter what your business sells, your customer wants to feel important. If they have a problem, they want to know you're there to help them solve it. They realize you're in business to make money, but you must earn that money by making them the priority.

That means taking a lesson from Trader Joe's. They don't just go above and beyond when there is a problem. From the smiling checkout guy to product quality, packaging, and return-anything policies, the commitment to their customers is always there, which is why their customers keep coming back.

Two

When Business Gets Personal

When A Visit To The Eye Doctor Gets On A Patient's Last Nerve

My eye was bothering me, so I went to the eye doctor. My regular doctor was not available, so I was given an appointment with someone else.

"Hello," she said with a very tight smile that stretched from one side of her mouth to the other but was not reflected in her eyes or facial muscles. "I'm Dr. Brown. What's the emergency?"

"I hope it's not an emergency," I replied.

"Well," she said, tapping her chart with her pen, "they put you in as an emergency, and I'm quite busy, so what's the problem?"

I felt a little pressure that was not just in my eye. She was obviously important, and I was taking up her valuable time.

"My guess is I have a floater or maybe a cataract," I explained. "But you're the doctor, so I'll let you tell me."

After a few questions and an eye examination to determine that my vision wasn't impaired, she put some drops in my eyes to dilate them and then called me back for a more thorough exam.

"Yep," she said, peering through a lens now stuck to my eye. "I see him. He's a floater all right."

"Really?" I asked. "What does he look like?" No answer. So I took a different approach, hoping to take advantage of her expertise: "What exactly is a floater?"

"It's a posterior vitreous detachment."

"What's that?" I asked.

"It's when the vitreous membrane separates from the retina," she said.

This was like pulling teeth, only I wasn't in the dentist's chair.

"So what is the vitreous membrane?" I asked. She explained that it's kind of like a gel in the middle of your eye that leaks fluid.

"That sounds serious," I said.

"Listen," she said, "You're my fifth floater today. To me, it's like bread and butter. It's not a big deal."

"But it is to me," I answered. "I've never had a floater and don't understand what it is. Can it get worse, or will it go away?"

"It won't go away," she said, "but you will get used to it."

"How will I get used to a little black spot floating in and out of my eye?" I wanted to understand.

"Look," she said, smiling again without really smiling. "It's like my underwear."

What? I wasn't sure I'd heard correctly, but she continued. "This morning, when I put on my underwear, I could feel it, but after wearing it for a while, I no longer knew it was there."

Okay. I wasn't fond enough of this woman to start picturing her in her underwear. And while I frequently urge speakers to use analogies to help listeners understand complicated information, I would not suggest that they speak about their undergarments.

She said I didn't have to worry about it unless I suddenly started seeing flashes of light. Concerned because I was traveling the next day, I asked what I should do if I had a problem.

Clearly exasperated at having to explain this bread-and-butter concept to the fifth person that day, she asked me where I was going.

"To Massachusetts," I said.

"They have excellent eye care in Massachusetts," she said. "If you see any flashes or have pain, you can go to a hospital there." How reassuring.

Then I saw the parallel in her message or lack of it to any of us who must communicate. It doesn't matter if you've given the same talk a thousand times. It's likely the first time your audience or listener has heard the information, and you should deliver it with the same gusto and enthusiasm you did the first time.

Second, it's your responsibility as a professional to speak to customers, clients, and any audience as if you genuinely care about their concerns and are truly interested in trying to solve their problems.

Finally, get over yourself. We know you're important, but so are we. We know you're smart, but so are we.

Your job as a professional is to help others. Your job as a communicator is to facilitate understanding. They go hand in hand. And, like the doctor's underwear, if you're genuine, you don't even have to think about it. It just happens naturally, as it should.

A Lesson On First Impressions: You Lost Me At "Hello"

It was a raw, rainy morning when I decided to leave the car at home and take the train into town. Normally, I would have walked to my destination, but given the miserable weather and the fact that I was lugging a couple of bags, walking nearly a mile through the wet streets of Philadelphia didn't seem like an enjoyable task. So I hailed a cab.

Imagine my surprise when the driver threw up his hands and grunted in disgust when I gave him the address. "It's right down there," he said, pointing.

"I know it's just a short ride," I said, "but it's pouring, and I have a lot to carry."

Then he yelled at me. "You need to be considerate of taxi drivers!"

No longer wanting his ride, I offered to take another cab, but he quickly pulled out, muttering words I didn't understand. And just in case I dared to question who was in charge, when I paid the fare and asked for change, he refused to give it to me. I wasn't about to argue.

As a homegrown Philly girl, I'm used to fanatic Eagles fans and sometimes harried East Coast behavior. But, for the most part, Philadelphians are warm, friendly people who take great pride in their city.

What if I had been visiting from out of town and that cab driver was my first impression of Philadelphia? How might I unfairly stereotype Philadelphians in general? What if I were a big-deal meeting planner who was so offended that she decided not to hold a large meeting here? Or a business manager looking for new office space who decided to look elsewhere? Maybe the driver picked up a film scout who changed his mind about shooting a movie here. Think of the repercussions: lost hotel, restaurant, and retail revenues, to name a few.

A single taxi driver has more clout than he or she may realize. Facial expressions, tone, attitude, and choice of words can quickly shape someone's impression of an entire city. Anything short of a welcoming, friendly attitude is simply bad PR, and bad PR is something most cities can hardly afford.

The lesson also spills over to the workplace, where hiring managers say that people form impressions about others within thirty seconds of meeting them. Some believe that candidates are mentally hired or not within the first ten minutes of an initial meeting. Contributing to those impressions are appearance, manners, and how the candidate treats assistants and receptionists. After all, the person behind the counter often has a direct line to the boss. If you're rude or condescending, his or her judgment of how you may or may not fit into the workplace could cost you the job.

Those of us who travel can likely recall a nasty airport employee you may have encountered on arrival, a surly cop who wasn't helpful when you asked for directions, or an unpleasant encounter with a shopkeeper. These experiences linger long after the trip is over. If the subject of that trip happens to come up in conversation, you may share a story about that rude taxi driver or nasty person who has become synonymous with the city or town you visited. And the bad PR continues.

Organizations spend good money with firms like ours to teach professionals and spokespeople how to make a great impression when they speak. While that's clearly important, it's often public servants and other front-line employees who are the faces of our communities. The impressions they leave behind are hard to put a price on.

She Wanted A Suck-Up And Didn't Find One. How Do You Teach Media Relations?

The woman left a voice mail at the office that went something like this: "Hi. We may have a need for your services sometime in the near future. I hear from your voice mail that you're on vacation, but regardless, I would like you to call me today."

So let me get this right. You're not a client. We don't know you. We have no clue who you work for or what your name is, and it doesn't appear that this is an emergency, but you're comfortable issuing instructions. I was out of the country on vacation, which is why my personal voice mail left my assistant's number and gave my e-mail address should someone need to reach me in an emergency before I returned.

When I retrieved the voice mail a few days later, I immediately called the woman. She said she had hoped I would have reached her sooner, but they had been conducting interviews, and "no one was right for this job," so we may still have a chance. She said she'd like to set up a call first thing in the morning. When I told her I wasn't available until later in the day and asked her to give me a brief sense of what she was calling about, she said, since that was the earliest I was available, I could wait to find out more.

That was probably the point in time I should have told this potential new client that I wasn't interested in her business. Giving orders to people who don't work for you is even more offensive than listening to commands from clients who are actually paying you. But I took the polite route and told her I was looking forward to learning more about her needs.

Several hours later, I received a strange calendar invite from someone I didn't know from a foundation I'd never heard of inviting me to participate in an hour-long program in a different time zone. Not having any idea of the relation between the two and thinking it was probably spam, I declined the invite. That's when the phone rang.

"This is so and so from the such and such foundation. When we e-mailed earlier today, you said you would be happy to talk to us at 4:00 p.m. tomorrow, and then I received this rude, nasty e-mail declining our invitation."

Aha! Now it clicked. The invite was from this same woman, who'd never told me the name of her organization and left a voice mail at the office. I was being given a second chance to decline potentially working with Ms. Insolent, but, trying to be polite and professional, I apologized for not realizing the directive was from her and confirming I'd be available. Then I hung up and went online to learn more about her organization.

The next day, at call time, with four others on the line and not coming up for air, she began to fill me in on the background. At first pause, I told her that I had done some homework and read a few articles about their organization.

"What did you read, and where did you read it?" she said.

I said I Googled them, and a bunch of things popped up that I perused. She informed me that anything I found online was inaccurate. She went on to say that her team needed help securing media exposure, but there was no media in her town. She said they reached out to several reporters directly, but only one called them back. When she said she wanted to read the story for approval before it was print- ed, he said no, so she didn't want to work with him.

I should have stopped there and realized I had been given a third chance to escape The Commander. Instead, I tried to be helpful. I explained that we were a communications coaching firm and could help craft messages and teach spokespeople how to speak to the me- dia, but I recommended she hire a public relations firm for story placement.

I explained that, because the story was about a philanthropist who died and dedicated his massive fortune to educating underprivileged children, regardless of the lack of media outlets, they could generate a lot of interest outside of their small town. I confirmed that reporters typically won't let you approve their story in advance.

To that, she said, "You can't meet our needs" and hung up.

A part of me wanted to send her an e-mail telling her that her atti- tude would kill any positive media coverage she hoped to generate and that she should hire us, as she clearly needs communications coach- ing. While an e-mail like that would have made me feel somewhat vindicated, it would have only continued a conversation I should have stopped before it started.

This woman clearly had no interest in anyone's advice. She was looking for a suck-up to agree with her point of view and do exactly what she wanted.

> ## She was looking for a suck up to agree with her point of view and do exactly what she wanted

In the workplace, this type of behavior creates an atmosphere of me versus you. These types of managers typically only invite input from others so they can challenge opinions and shoot them down. Instead of involving people, they alienate them, which robs the entire company of fresh ideas and different ways of doing things.

If I had sent Ms. Insolent that e-mail, I might have offered the following media advice, which applies in the workplace as well:

- If you want media coverage, take the time to understand what the media needs so they can help you succeed. If you want motivated employees and loyal customers, don't dictate. Converse.
- When you welcome different viewpoints, you generate conversations filled with interesting information that can lead to new ideas and valuable contributions.
- Embracing those ideas often helps attract talented, creative people who have your best interest at heart.

Finally, people who truly want your help will ask for it. If they don't ask, they're probably more interested in the sound of their own voice than your help. Maybe you can't meet their needs, as Ms. Insolent stated, but if one of your basic needs is to be treated with respect, they can't meet your needs either.

When E-Mail Sends The Wrong Signal

The training program went so well that one of the participants e-mailed me, gushing about how much she learned. So much that she wanted to get together for lunch to "pick my brain." I wasn't sure what that meant, but said, "Sure, give me a call."

I'm not a big let's-have-lunch person. Because of the nature of our business, I'm often not in the office, and when I am, I need the time to prepare for upcoming engagements. After accounting for travel time and lunch time, lunch frequently means taking a half day off. However, I didn't want to turn her down and send the wrong message. She was respectful and told me she valued my time, and because she was located an hour from me, she would pick a restaurant close to my office.

When her assistant e-mailed a meeting invite several weeks later, I accepted. A few days before our meeting, she cancelled. The assistant rescheduled, and she cancelled again. I offered to schedule a call instead. She said she'd rather meet in person. Two months later, lunch was rescheduled again.

As the date approached, she e-mailed, asking me to find a restaurant in an area about forty minutes away from my office, which she said would be easier for her to get to that day. Annoyed that she apparently forgot she respected my time and unfamiliar with the neighborhood, I reached out to some colleagues for recommendations, but no one had any.

Trying to be cooperative, I suggested several alternative places that were closer to both of us. She e-mailed me back with another suggestion that required even more travel time for both of us.

My exact response was, "Sure, though I think that's probably farther for both of us. Whatever works is fine. See you tomorrow."

Yet, when tomorrow came, I was greeted with this early morning e-mail: "Karen, maybe I have a misunderstanding. Aren't we a client of yours? I am surprised about how difficult it is to arrange a simple lunch. This is not urgent or pressing. I was hoping to engage you for some services with my team. I don't think that it's going to work out at this point. We can let lunch go for now."

Dumbfounded, I stared at the e-mail and then read it again to make sure I was reading it correctly. Upset that she was upset but irritated at her response, I called, got her voice mail, and left an apology. Then I e-mailed her back, saying, "I profusely apologize and did not mean to make this difficult. I'm happy to meet you for lunch wherever you like. I was trying to be accommodating by finding something closer to both of us but clearly sent the wrong message."

She never responded. So what went wrong?

E-mails, while quick and easy, have no tone, so they can be easily misunderstood. When you talk to people in person or over the phone, they see facial expressions, hear the inflection in your voice, and sense emotional connections to topics. However, a seemingly innocent remark or comment that might be funny in person could be completely misunderstood in an e-mail.

A study published in the *Journal of Personality and Social Psychology* found that people interpret the tone and mood of an e-mail only 50 percent of the time. That means you might be pleased, but the e-mail recipient perceives you're not. It's these types of misinterpretations that lead to arguments, harm productivity, and turn people against each other in the workplace.

Had my fan turned foe and I connected by phone to agree on a lunch place, perhaps our mix-up would have been avoided.

Yet, in today's global workplace, phone conversations to schedule meetings are not always possible, and thanks to technology, scheduling lunch no longer requires a phone call. Here are five tips to help you avoid unintended e-mail snafus:

- Don't assume what someone else means. If you're not sure, pick up the phone and call.
- Don't bury the lede. For example, instead of saying, "The client wants the top of this presentation reworked to better reflect the message," say, "You did a great job on this presentation, but the client wants us to work on tightening the very top." This way, the receiver hears "you did a great job" first.
- Consider the relationship. If someone knows you well, he or she is more in tune with your communication style and less likely to take offense or misinterpret your words. If not, it's easier for your communication to be misread.
- Consider the person. If you know people well, you have a better understanding of their personality and what might upset them.
- Re-read. Before hitting Send, re-read the e-mail to see if it's laced with tone or mood that could be misconstrued.

In my case, perhaps the e-mail recipient sensed I didn't really want to have lunch even though I didn't actually say that. Or maybe she was dealing with other issues and simply took her bad mood out on me.

Whatever the case, there is a common expression: "It takes two to tango." That means, regardless of intent or excuse, we are both responsible for the outcome.

It's Never Too Late To Be The Person You Want Others To See

I pulled into the parking lot clogged with construction vehicles with five minutes to spare. The client had asked me to work with their chairman of the board, so being late would not make a great first impression.

Turning the corner, I eyed a rare open spot halfway down the crowded row. As I sped up and signaled to move in, a big black Infiniti coming from the opposite direction signaled the same. Our cars inched up with no room to turn, and we both stopped. He wasn't budging, and neither was I. So we sat staring at each other through the windshields. I knew I was about to be late, but I wasn't giving in. I could wait this out if he could. I took my foot off the brake and pushed in to park.

Tick tock, the minutes passed. Then, finally, he couldn't take any more. Throwing his car into reverse, he muttered something I couldn't hear and screeched out of the row. I pulled into the coveted space. Victory was worth the wait. Or was it?

As I triumphantly strode to the front door, something dawned on me. What if the guy driving the black Infiniti were the chair? *No*, I told myself, *stop being paranoid*. But somewhere in my gut, as I walked down the hallway into the boardroom, I knew this was how the story would play out.

I opened the door, and there was Infiniti Man, sitting in a chair, arms crossed, staring me down. No one spoke. Now it was my turn to give in. "Where did you park?" I asked.

"You mean after you stole my spot?" he asked. More staring.

Then it was my turn to give in. I held out my hand and said, "Let's start over," and we did.

Have you ever botched a first impression? Perhaps you spilled coffee on someone's white shirt or forgot an important prospect's name. You've likely heard the cliché "You never get a second chance to make a good first impression." Perhaps that's true, but it's never too late to change initial impressions and be the person you want others to see. While you can't undo a faux pas, you can repair negative first impressions.

ADDRESS THE ELEPHANT IN THE ROOM

You can't move forward if you don't acknowledge what's on people's mind. Until you address what they care about, they won't be open to new ideas and information.

For example, I worked with a real estate developer who frequently addressed community meetings packed with angry people who don't want another housing development going up in their backyard. He said that, as soon as he started talking, people interrupted, argued, and shouted at him. As we worked together, it became apparent that he was so focused on explaining his objectives that he failed to adequately address audience concerns. When he reorganized his talk and spoke to their worries at the onset, they were much more receptive to hearing his plans.

APOLOGIZE WHEN NECESSARY

Not every situation requires an apology, but if you've offended someone unintentionally, focusing on being right instead of repositioning your words will only make things worse. So apologize quickly and look for cues. Does the person's body language and facial expression indicate acceptance of your apology? Try to avoid overapologizing, which can make the other person uncomfortable and not allow the conversation to move on.

How can you tell whether your first impression or corrected first impression was well received?

A study at conducted by researchers at Washington University in St. Louis and Wake Forest University in North Carolina suggests that self-confidence makes all the difference when knowing whether you've hit a home run or struck out with your first impression. They found that, if you're confident in your judgment of the situation, you're likely to be right. In other words, trust your gut. When you don't, you can misjudge how others see you and make the wrong assumption.

DON'T ASSUME HOW OTHERS FEEL

That's why it's critical to share how you feel and not suggest how you think your impression affected someone. For example, instead of saying, "I know you probably think I'm a real jerk for taking that parking space," you defuse the uncomfortable situation by saying, "I feel terrible about our first encounter and realize I may not have seen your blinker on."

While we don't get second chances to make first impressions, we always have opportunities to make lasting impressions that are created and honed over time.

When Business Gets Personal

When you do something stupid, you know you're doing it as you're doing it. This was the case with me as I was watching a nationally televised town hall meeting featuring the two presidential candidates. I make it a practice not to publicly voice my political opinions, as our client base is diversified, and my personal preferences have nothing to do with our ability to work together.

On this particular night, for whatever reason, my stupid gene got the better of me. Annoyed at the interviewer's line of questioning, I tweeted a criticism of the interviewer to my followers. Seconds later, a client privately replied, "I saw your tweet. Which political candidate did you think was being treated unfairly?" I made the mistake of answering.

The corporate communications director at this well-respected firm has been a trusted colleague for nearly two decades. I've spoken at many of the company's corporate events, and our team has provided ample consultation and coaching. I was tentatively scheduled to speak at their upcoming corporate retreat—that is, until the morning after my tweet, when I received an e-mail from my client. It told me to release the date, as they'd decided to go in a different direction.

Really? A different direction? Why couldn't they just say, "We disagree with your political position, which is different from ours, and that's why we've decided not to work with you"? Assuming that's the reason, it would have been more truthful, even if it's not politically correct.

Tweeting was stupid and perhaps unprofessional. Given I tell my clients, colleagues and my husband not to post personal viewpoints on social media, I should know better. Yet I would never fire someone for having an opposing viewpoint.

From gun control to immigration to abortion rights to a host of other hot-button issues, my graphic artist and I are on opposite sides of the political fence. Yet I consistently hire him because he's great at what he does. From Pennsylvania to Texas, we've had lengthy discussions about our differences and agree to disagree because we know we'll never agree. However, we still respect each other's professional opinions and move on.

This client couldn't get past my tweet, not because I tweeted but because I am diametrically opposed to his beliefs, which he has shared with me in the past. That's unfortunate because we have done great work together and always enjoyed working together.

In most cases, mixing personal viewpoints with business relationships isn't a recommended recipe. In business, people expect an outside advisor to offer expert advice even if it's contrary. They want your experienced insight no matter how unconventional. That's what they pay you for. Voicing your unsolicited opinion on personal matters is an entirely different story.

In that case, if they want your opinion, they'll ask for it.

Three

VALUE YOUR VALUES

Value Your Values

I was waiting for a train when I ran into a big celebrity. We've known each other for years. When I was a television reporter who covered his comings and goings, he gushed at my presence. When I ran for political office, he contributed to my campaign and even called on occasion. When I wrote a book, he was happy to be quoted and see his name in print. Yet, recently, when I walked up to him with a big hello and an outstretched hand, he barely acknowledged me, saying, "Oh, hi, nice to see you," and then quickly walked away.

At first, I was surprised. Surprise turned to annoyance. Annoyance turned to offence. Then I realized caring at all was a waste of energy. Most of us have come across people like this. They welcome you with open arms when they think you are in a position to help or possibly hurt them. When you no longer hold those cards, they discard you like a used tissue. Their former smiles, grandiose gestures, and attentiveness were never sincere to begin with.

My psychologist friend classifies many of these people as narcissists, people who believe the world revolves around them. She says they tend to be charming but use their charm to get what they want. She says they often have a sense of entitlement and have no problem taking advantage of others, which can be dangerous both personally and professionally.

By now, you're probably thinking of someone you know who fits that description and perhaps wondering what you can do about his or her behavior if it's affecting you or others in the workplace.

For starters, understand that most of these people probably don't realize or care that you consider their behavior inappropriate, as they do not share your values. So you have three choices:

1. You can ignore their conduct and kiss up to them because you think you need them.
2. You can develop strategies to deal with them, especially if you must interact with them in the workplace.
3. You can avoid them completely.

Years ago, we received an urgent Saturday afternoon call from a CEO begging for help. His company was about to take a public beating. His reputation was at stake, and he wanted us to help strategize the right way to approach the problem and communicate to different stakeholders, specifically the media. We dropped everything to work through the weekend and then some. When all was said and done, the negative coverage was minimal, and his public problems went away.

Yet, when we sent a bill, he didn't pay the full amount. Thinking it was an honest mistake, I called him and learned he'd paid less on purpose. During the event, he asked us to stretch the truth at someone else's expense, which we would not do. Despite the quick positive results, he said he wasn't satisfied because we didn't agree to his demands. Stunned, we never recovered the money but learned never to work with people who do not share our core values.

I know a highly paid professor who is adept at getting others to do her work for her. While she is paid to teach at an Ivy League institution, every week, she invites a subject expert to teach her class but does not pay the speaker. She claims she's giving these people opportunities and hints that, because she is well connected in business and politics, there will be professional payoffs down the road. I used to buy this and conducted classes as well as provided free counsel for her many times until I realized I was being used. When I stopped accepting engagements, she asked why, so I told her the truth. She told me I was making a mistake.

Today, she is in a powerful position, and we no longer work together. People have questioned why I won't rekindle the relationship when she could throw big contracts our way. Some have advised me to step down from my moral high horse and go with option one: ignore her conduct. Others suggest that having strategies in place to interact with her is a wise compromise because it would keep the relationship with this powerful person intact.

I chose option three, to have nothing to do with her, which probably cost us some business and referrals. My reasoning is simple. We do not share the same values and ethics; therefore, she is not the right fit for our company, clients, or brand. When you betray your core values, you know it in your gut. You feel queasy, lose sleep, and can obsess over it.

But when you surround yourself with partners, friends, and colleagues who share your values, you feel more grounded. In Shakespeare's *Hamlet*, Polonius told his son, "To thine own self be true."

When we fail to listen to our inner voice, not only can we ignore our values and deceive ourselves but we can also mislead those who believe in us.

Little White Lies: Sifting The Good From The Bad

My mother and I have ongoing battles with our scales. In her case, sometimes she doesn't like what it says. She fiddles with it, adjusts how she places her feet, changes the batteries, and gets on and off it several times, determined to find her desired weight. When she gets totally disgusted with the scale, she returns it to the store and purchases a new one because the extra pounds are clearly the fault of the scale.

Come to think of it, my mother's mother had scale issues too. She simply said it was wrong and got off. My scale can also be off sometimes. However, I find, if I move it slightly to the left or to the right, I can actually shave off a half pound, and on a good day, if I center it just right, I can even lose a full pound. So when my scale says I've gained a few, I am confident the real problem is its location on my bathroom floor. Or perhaps it's simply a genetic trait inherited from my mother's side of the family.

Scaling back the pounds made me wonder how we balance the lies that we tell privately and publicly. What's the difference between deluding yourself and deluding others? If I move my scale to make myself feel better, who am I really hurting? But if management deludes themselves into believing things are better than they really are, then they might not take corrective actions when needed. Self-deceit can affect stock price and morale and grind a company to a halt.

There are other whoppers that turn into public scandals. Athletes have lied about drug use. Politicians lie about money and extramarital affairs. Job applicants embellish resumes. People post book and product reviews when they haven't read the book or used the product.

Researchers have been studying the topic of lying for decades, and it turns out we bend the truth a lot. We ask people how they're doing when we don't really care. We fib about weight and the size of our clothing. We post profile pictures on social sites that make us look decades younger than we really are. We tell friends and family members we loved their gift even though we've already sold it on eBay.

Companies spin news every day. They promise products that will make you look ten years younger and twist negatives into positive headlines.

In fact, lying is so prevalent that one study reported most of us lie once a day and that 60 percent of people lie at least once in a ten-minute conversation. Published articles suggest we learn how to tell tales as early as three years old, often mimicking our parents. Most parents don't deliberately teach us to lie, but we observe them stretching the truth to protect someone else's feelings.

Whether well intended or not, all this fibbing makes it difficult to tell fact from fiction. That can be serious in business, where fudging facts can have significant repercussions.

A study published in the *Harvard Business Review* found that people with power seem to have a greater ability to deceive others. They divided research subjects into two groups: bosses and employees. Half the subjects were instructed to steal a one-hundred-dollar bill. If they could convince an interviewer they hadn't taken it, they could keep it. All the subjects, even those who didn't steal money, were questioned. In the interviews, lying bosses displayed fewer signs of dishonesty and stress and were harder to distinguish from those telling the truth.

So how can you tell if someone is lying?

Stanford's Graduate School of Business considered this when they conducted a study a few years ago. They analyzed the transcripts of nearly thirty thousand conference calls by American chief executives and chief financial officers and paid attention to how people deliver words differently when fibbing. The study suggested that bosses who lie avoid saying "I" and instead speak in the third person. It said they use stronger words like "fantastic" instead of "good" to sound more persuasive.

Lie detection experts say no single behavior will give someone away, but there are four nonverbal signs of deception: touching hands, touching the face, crossing the arms, and leaning away.

As an example, in our company's speaker coaching sessions, we observe that, when people share stories and personal experiences, they are usually lively and use their hands to express themselves. If someone is lying or telling a story that didn't really happen, we notice that they gesture less and their facial expressions are typically not as animated.

So when is lying okay? If your partner asks, "Do I look fat in this?," and you think so, telling the truth may result in hurt feelings. And what about the four-year-old who believes in Santa Claus? Telling the child Santa isn't real may spoil the youthful allure of Christmas. If someone asks you to do something followed by, "Do you mind?" and you say you don't even though you might mind a little, is that kind of a lie bad?

Perhaps what we need to do is differentiate between harmless lies that are meant to protect someone else and more serious lies that are about protecting ourselves at the expense of others.

By the way, my mom just called. She got a new scale.

Careful Not To Trip Over Your Own Power

Power tripping. The Urban Dictionary defines it as "someone, typically at work, who has higher powers over most people they work with" whose power tends to go to his or her head, causing such people to abuse their rights as a boss just because they can.

We all know people like this. Self-important, self-absorbed, and self-impressed. They use their power to get what they want at the expense of others and to remind themselves of their greatness.

I was engaged by a power-tripping client just this week. We had completed a corporate communications training, but the tripper who happened to hire us said the business office required some additional information if we wanted to get paid. After numerous back and forth e-mails with the client, who couldn't explain what the business office actually wanted, she forwarded their e-mail to me, copied them, and instructed me to provide what was requested.

Only the forwarded e-mail was laced with a lot of mumbo jumbo such as "no reference to the governing paper" and questions about pricing being standard fees or broken down and altered to reference government agreements. I didn't understand it. So, given she copied the person in charge of paying us on her e-mail to me, I e-mailed that person directly, making sure to copy my client, thinking she'd appreciate my effort. I couldn't have been more wrong.

Moments later, a terse e-mail from her appeared in my inbox ordering me to communicate only with her on this matter and not to speak to anyone else. But wait, didn't she copy them on her e-mail to me? Did I do something wrong?

No. Anyone who spends enough time with people knows that some will pull rank to show power. According to Dr. Ilona Jerabek, president of Psych Tests, "What a lot of people don't realize is, when you pull rank to make sure people do what you want them to do, you lose some of that power."

> Like school yard bullies, grown up power trippers have simply graduated to the role of office bullies

It occurred to me that, like school yard bullies, grown-up power trippers have simply graduated to the role of office bullies. They use their position to command authority and respect by letting others know they are in charge. Yet, as Dr. Jerabek pointed out, this need for control can cause the opposite effect and come at the expense of others.

As I mulled over the e-mail, willing myself not to be sucked into my client's power trip, I recalled something I observed at that training program that I would not have remembered if this recent correspondence hadn't taken place.

There was a participant the power tripper told me she didn't like. Smart, educated, and assertive, this person wasn't afraid to voice her opinion even if it conflicted with the power tripper, who held a higher rank. At the end of the program, when that participant asked a question to clarify information, the power tripper shot her down in front of everyone in the room. It was like watching a monkey beat its chest to show everyone who was in charge. The participant was humiliated and embarrassed in front of her peers.

Every one of us has the capacity to lead, but that doesn't make someone a good leader. Leading is about motivating, inspiring, communicating, and making others feel valued. When you degrade others, not only can you damage morale and productivity but you may unknowingly damage your own reputation as well, which ultimately could strip you of that power you so value.

Yet we can't always tattle like we did on the playground. What we can do is adapt a few *don't* strategies to trip up the tripper who wants you to engage.

DON'T PARTICIPATE

I wanted to return my client's e-mail with a nasty response. That would only make her angry and affect business we do company wide. So I answered politely and professionally, focusing only on discussing the information requested.

DON'T SINK TO THEIR LEVEL

If the power tripper says things like, "Do I have to do everything?" or "How many times do I have to tell you?," instead of insulting them back, ask for clarification, saying you want to make sure you understand so you can provide what is needed.

DON'T KEEP TALKING

The less you say, the less likely it is you'll be sucked into the tripper's trap. When you give the tripper too many words, you are supplying that person with ammunition to use against you.

As difficult as it may be, there are lessons to be learned from the power trippers in your life. While their behavior may be deplorable at times, you may learn how to be a better listener, how to develop strategies to adjust your own responses, and ways to hone your own personal leadership style based on what you don't like about the behavior of others.

That way, when you find yourself in a position of power, you might be a little extra careful not to trip yourself up by letting it go to your head.

As A Girl, She Lost Her Precious Watch But Learned A Valuable Lesson

When I was thirteen, a group of relatives bought me the most beautiful watch I had ever seen. It was dainty, the oval face dotted with diamonds and emeralds. I never wanted to take it off.

My mom said I could only wear it for special occasions, but before I did, she said it must be insured in case something happened.

At thirteen, I wondered what could possibly happen. At thirteen, my point of view was the only viewpoint that mattered. So when I dressed for a special party at a country club a few days later, I put it on. My parents were out for the evening, and I would be home before them, so they'd never know.

I was careful—*really* careful. I made sure the clasp was securely fastened, and I kept looking at my wrist every few minutes to make sure it was there. I even took it off in the ladies' room so I wouldn't get it wet when I washed my hands.

Only I forgot to put it back on. When I looked at my naked wrist a few moments later, I panicked. I ran back to the ladies' room. It wasn't there. I looked in every sink and under the stalls. I even rummaged through the trash. Not there either. I went to the front desk and told them what happened. They took my phone number and said they'd call if it showed up. It never did.

My parents were furious but didn't punish me. I was so upset about losing the watch that they probably thought that was punishment enough.

When I think back to that day some decades ago, I can still feel the panic in the pit of my stomach. It's a feeling that surfaces in all of us from time to time but for different reasons. Perhaps when we make a big mistake and try to cover it up or offend someone by saying something we shouldn't have said. Maybe we tell a white lie and fear the consequences. Or maybe we're worried about something that is totally out of our control.

In business, this is not productive. To lead, you must focus on the bigger picture, and that means taking time to understand different points of view. While you may not always agree or implement their ideas, you're communicating that you value their input, and that inspires confidence in others.

As a reporter for many years, it was my job to gather both sides of the story, which typically meant opposing viewpoints. I quickly learned that there are far more than two sides to every story, and to do justice to multiple opinions, I had to strive for balance.

Strong leaders must also balance opinions by thinking forward. That means continually evaluating how a decision made today may affect the future. It also means communicating to those around you if you hope they'll follow your lead. When you fail to consider the opinions of others, you end up talking to yourself, and that creates a false sense of reality.

While disobeying your parents at the young age of thirteen seems insignificant years later, the lessons learned carry into adulthood. For starters, many of us realize that adults often knew more than we gave them credit for. And for those of us who strive to have others follow our lead, we learn that we can't lead if the only viewpoint we consider is our own.

I've owned a lot of watches since that day so many years ago. Beautiful watches bought by my parents and watches given to me by my husband. I even have a watch my grandmother left to me that means the world to me. But nothing will ever replace the watch I lost even though the lesson learned was just as valuable.

Referrals Should Be Your Best Salespeople

On November twentieth, I sent an e-mail to a colleague I'll call Dawn. It read, "I just highly recommended you and passed your name on to a terrific client who is looking for the kind of services you provide. I hope it works out."

On January third, some six weeks later, I received this response: "It's great to hear from you! I apologize for the delayed response. If your client is still looking, I have someone on my team who can help."

Frankly, six weeks later, I didn't remember which client had asked for the referral. More importantly, six weeks later, why would I ever recommend business to her again when my referral was never even acknowledged? Additionally, Dawn's belated response made me realize I had never followed up with the client, which could have made me look bad.

If you've been in business long enough, then you know how important referrals are. They are a free way to market your services. Satisfied customers and others who think highly of your reputation are the best salespeople you could ever ask for. People are more likely to hire a firm based on recommendations from a trusted source than any other means. Even if a new client finds you on social media, they'll typically check you out through a mutual connection before considering your services.

The hallmark of building a successful business is continually delivering great value to all your clients so they talk about you. In our business, if you make a difference for one person at one company, that person will recommend you to someone else, who will recommend you to someone else. Before you know it, not only are you the go-to person at that company but you may find yourself working with hundreds of people at that business and possibly across the industry.

When you provide poor service or fail to acknowledge the kindness of others, people also talk. In fact, they talk more when they're angry or unhappy. It doesn't take very long for their negative opinion of you to spread. Combine that with social media and online review sites, and complaints can put you out of business.

It's also important to understand that referrals spark more referrals. Just yesterday, I received a call from the head of communications at a global company. The conversation went something like this: "Hi, Karen. I received your name from Sallie Smith, who speaks very highly of you. We're looking for a communications firm to work with our sales team and hope you are available."

Thanks to Sallie, they were sold on our company before we even spoke.

Here's what you might find even more interesting. I recalled Sallie's name, but wasn't exactly sure who she was, so I looked her up on LinkedIn and discovered I had never worked with her but had worked with her colleagues about six years ago, when she was climbing the ladder at a different company. Since then, she's moved twice, and both times, we were brought into those companies, though I never realized she was the connection.

So I sent her an e-mail thanking her for thinking of us. Her response? "It's my pleasure. You are always at the top of my list."

That's a good list to be on. Sallie heads global corporate communications for a company that has more than twelve thousand employees worldwide.

While it would be nice to send people who refer you a token or handwritten note, it's not required, and most professionals aren't recommending you in hopes of getting a gift. If others are happy with your work, you just made the person who referred you look good. Sometimes, people who don't even know you continually recommend you because they've heard good things, and you're the only person they know who does what you do.

That is partly the case with Dawn, whom I referenced at the top of this article. I don't know many people who do what she does, but I've known her for nearly twenty-five years, and she has a good reputation. So, when I was asked if I knew someone who does what she does, her name was always at the top of my list. My referrals have turned into some of her clients.

As I think about Dawn, I recall that, over the years, she has occasionally contacted me for advice and asked for introductions to people I know. I was happy to oblige.

Even if she didn't want the business, she should have immediately followed up with a brief e-mail or phone call acknowledging my referral and appreciating any time or effort I'd put forth on her behalf.

The next time someone you know or don't know sings your praises, treat them the way you'd want to be treated if you want them to continue saying good things about your services.

I wish Dawn well; however, I'll never refer her again. One less referral might be trivial to her, but it is significant to me. I'd rather risk not being able to help someone than being embarrassed by providing a referral that I can't follow up on.

Advice To A Younger Self

I take nothing for granted. When I left my career of more than twenty years as a broadcaster, I was scared. Not about the future but about losing perspective. As a reporter, I spent my fair share of hours with people born into less fortunate circumstances than myself.

I learned so much from them. Humility. Honesty. Tenacity. Survival.

So, when I chose to leave broadcasting and forge a new path two decades ago, I feared that not spending time in not-so-nice neighborhoods with people who experienced the world differently from me might turn me into someone who doesn't appreciate what I have as much as I should.

I know a lot of people born and raised in great environments who go on to do great things. Partly because they have the means and partly because of their fortunate birth circumstances.

Whom we are born to often dictates who we become. Yes, there are thousands of stories about people who overcome the odds, and they should be applauded because those odds were stacked against them at birth.

Years ago, we spent Christmas dinner with the family of close friends. One of the relatives was a prominent surgeon at a pediatric hospital. He remarked that we are all born into this world equally. I disagreed, and unfortunately, a holiday argument ensued. He said every one of us has an equal chance to pave our own way. I argued that being born to a crack addict in a crime-ridden neighborhood with no nurturing, mentors, or money does not afford people the same access to education, contacts, and opportunities. He said a person's desire to achieve is in their DNA. I said I was glad he wasn't my doctor.

I never forgot that conversation because he was the person I feared becoming. Someone entitled. Someone sheltered. Someone self-absorbed. Someone unaware and unappreciative of people's differences.

Today, I run a business. Fortunately, we do well, but not a day goes by that I fear the phone might not ring or a deal might dissolve. When I share my insecurities with close colleagues, they chuckle and reassure me that, at this point my career, I have nothing to worry about.

If I didn't worry, that might be true. But I believe that those who worry work harder. Those who fear failure never take success for granted. Those who stagnate and accept the status quo stop moving forward.

Sometimes I contemplate how I got here. It's fun and really cool. We have great clients. The calendar is full. But when self-appreciation begins to runs amok, I try to dial it back and take a serious reality check.

I was born to great role models who provided, nurtured, guided, and offered opportunities that others may not have received. Yes, I worked hard. I've been employed since I was fourteen. I still work tirelessly for every nugget of success. Maybe that is part of my DNA, but I take nothing for granted.

Like many business owners, I've gone through dry times and scary times. But I'm blessed to do what I love and call it work. I could be working at any number of unsatisfactory jobs earning basic wages and struggling to make ends meet. I could be unemployed. Or sick. Or alone. But I'm not. That's something I'll never take for granted because, the moment I do, I may not appreciate those who have so much less.

If I had understood then what I appreciate now, this is the advice I would give a younger self embarking on a career:

- **Treat everyone the same.** Realize that we are born to different circumstances, but everyone has something to offer the world.
- **Stay true to yourself.** Surround yourself with people who share your values.
- **Follow your passion.** If that means getting a night job to allow you to do what you love, do it. It will never feel like work.
- **Grow and improve.** This allows you to continually share your knowledge and become someone who is focused on helping others.

Finally, take nothing for granted, and you will always appreciate where you came from and look forward to where you're going.

Four

PERFORMANCE

Moving The Why-I-Should-Care Dial

The new client was a small start-up company. I was brought in to help them explain how their rather complicated product could benefit various stakeholders, including the media. From my vantage point, I wanted them to learn how to move the why-should-I-care dial.

The first person to enter room was the president and CEO, who didn't say hello but asked, "Where is the escape route?"

"Escape route?" I asked. "Are you planning to leave?"

"It depends on how your session is," he said. "I typically don't like these things."

"Have you ever attended media training?"

"No," he said, "but the media is wrong all the time, and I already know how to talk about what we do."

"Well," I said as the rest of the group entered the room, "good media training is good communications training, and perhaps you'll learn something you didn't know."

"Maybe," he said, "but I doubt it."

This is a man who leads his young company and product to success. Aside from poor manners, his arrogance, ego, negative attitude, and sour tone filled the room like a stale aroma.

I was seething and wanted to put him in his place. How dare he undermine my credibility in front of the people I'm supposed to educate before the day even began? My first instinct was to go toe to toe with him. But a quick recalculation of my internal thermometer reminded me to take advice I might give a client and focus on setting an example, which meant applying positive communication skills.

So I backed off, realizing the best way to show this know-it-all what he didn't know was to let him show himself.

We began a series of video-recorded mock media interviews. I was playing a business reporter. He went first, as he "didn't have much time for this" and needed to leave early.

I asked what his company did, and he responded with words like "target markets," "value proposition," "aggregate and analyze," and "apply data management to create platforms for care coordination." I tried to stay awake.

"What exactly does that mean?" I asked. With his arms crossed defensively, he talked about bridging gaps, monetary drivers, and quality in health care provision.

So I pressed further, reminding him that the people reading my mock publication were primarily hospital executives. Even though these words may be accurate, they do not address how his company can bridge gaps, improve quality, and save money.

He said I didn't get it and left the room.

I'll tell you what I do get. Stories, presentations, and communications are not about you. They're about what matters to a reader, viewer, or audience. No one cares how smart you are or how impressive your vocabulary is. They don't need to know everything you know. People want to know how your information benefits or affects them. How can you solve their problems? What will improve or change because of your product or service? If you really want people to buy what you're selling, then sell the outcome.

> If you really want people to buy what you're selling, then sell the outcome

This company helps patients transition from hospital to home. Technology enables all their information to be easily accessed by clinicians, caretakers, and others involved in their care so they know what medicines to take, when to schedule follow-up appointments, and what to do if they get sick again. This reduces hospital readmissions, costs, frees up beds, and provides better care. That's the outcome. That's what the reader cares about.

Interestingly, as soon as the CEO walked out of the room, the atmosphere dramatically changed. His subordinates who co-founded the company wanted more. They are good people who passionately believe in their product and through continued exercises recognized that they don't know how to explain what they are selling. They conceded that they make what they do sound too complicated and fear they could be outmaneuvered by competitors who offer solutions that appear simpler.

The exercise with their leader reinforced the need to develop people-centric messages that humanize information so people would care about what they were saying. Through additional mock interviews, they recognized that sometimes just a tiny change in wording can transform how a message is received. They were very excited and ended the day eager to get together again so they could continue to move forward.

That would have been great, but the next day, the CEO banned agencies and other expert communicators. He said they didn't understand his business.

There is a difference between leading and dictating. Strong leaders embrace ideas and opinions and are open to seeing things differently. They thrive on creativity, which leads to innovation and strong partnerships. Dictators aren't interested in what others say. It's all about them, and their massive egos drive their decisions.

When companies are run by dictators, there are usually an abundance of escape seats. Unfortunately, the escapees are customers, investors, and employees.

Let Me Tell You A Story About Steve From The Coffee Shop

His name is Steve. He's retired now, but before spending mornings at the local coffee shop, he spent forty years in sales, owned his own company, and boasted a resume of successes.

For a good ten years now, I've enjoyed a morning cup of joe with Steve and a small group of loyal Manhattan Bagel regulars in my neighborhood. Sometimes it's a quick buy and bye. Other times, we sit and chat. We've sipped through elections and wars, simmered over political differences, and added extra sweetener to sugarcoat a disappointing Philadelphia Eagles loss. We've come to value each other's opinions even if, like a steaming cup of coffee, our differences sometimes bubble over.

So, on this fall morning, I asked Steve to share his secret of sales success. Without hesitation, he answered, "Ask for the order" and then added, "Let me tell you a story." Without realizing the full impact of those six words—let me tell you a story—Steve shared the secret ingredient of his years of sales success. He's a natural, engaging storyteller. From heroic saves on the tennis court to his grandchildren's antics at holiday dinners, he has a knack for using quick stories to create an emotional connection that makes "the ask" relevant to the listener's life.

Consider this. At a communications training program for pharmaceutical sales representatives, repeated role-playing revealed that these seasoned pros knew everything there was to know about their product, disease, and challenges faced by both health care providers and patients. However, because their real-life face time with prospects is so limited, they said they felt pressured to quickly rattle off information in monologue style without pausing to ask questions and better understand their listeners' concerns. They were focused on what they wanted to say instead of engaging their listeners. They said they didn't have time to tell stories.

Oscar-winning producer and business author Peter Guber reminds us that "hits are made in the heart, not in the head." Stories can be short quips or quick examples that reinforce facts and help listeners understand why they should care. When we use stories to illustrate points, we increase attention and retention because we invite listeners to become active participants.

As I was writing this article, I received an e-mail from one of the reps who attended that communications training. She said that, after seeing the difference in how her peers perceived her during role-playing, she decided to practice her newfound storytelling skills at a sales call. Not only did a heartfelt story about a patient strike a chord with her client but he told her he now considers her and her company a valuable resource. He trusts them.

The next time you try to make a sale, think of the story you want people to hear. How would you tell it over a quick cup of coffee?

In our coaching programs, we challenge people to answer the "so what?" by coming up with prove-it examples that have solved customers' problems. For example, a financial services executive shared a story about a customer who was declined a loan after forty-five years with the same local bank. He explained how his company was able to quickly and easily secure a loan for the man, which ultimately resulted in significant business growth. Instead of sounding promotional or conceited, the prove-it example answered the "so what?" and offered the customer concrete reasons to understand why his company was a good fit.

One of the biggest mistakes we observe when working with sales staff or other spokespeople is the following misperception: my listener understands what I'm talking about. Just because your listener is part of your world doesn't mean they understand your business or product or know what you know. If you assume your customers understand the problem and they don't, you've lost a huge opportunity to influence them, and as Steve would do, go for the ask.

As I swallowed the last of my coffee and readied to leave my table with Steve, the man behind the bagel counter yelled, "Would you like any bagels today?"

I replied, "No thanks, Elliot."

"Okay," he said, "but they're hot, right out of the oven."

"Come to think of it," I answered, "I'll take two. One for Steve and one for me. And by the way, thanks for asking."

Speakers: Do Your Audience A Favor And Get Over Yourself

I was really excited to hear the speaker. She's a well-known network correspondent whom I've watched for years. She's thought provoking and witty and quickly cuts to the chase. So when I changed my flight to get to the conference in time to hear her speak, imagine my disappointment when she blew it. Actually, I was more disappointed that she had no clue she blew it.

Here she was—a media celebrity in a ballroom of seasoned public relations professionals, but she had not stopped to consider her audience and what they cared about. Yes, she told a few stories about life in the news trenches, but the stories were all about her. How great she was. The obstacles she had to overcome. The tough decisions she makes every day. Me, me, me, and more me.

What she failed to do was help her audience understand how they could use this information. What lessons did she learn that her listeners could apply to their lives? How could her vignettes empower, motivate, or inspire others to action? Most importantly, how could they benefit from her expertise and apply it to their profession so they could maximize results?

Just because you talk on TV or find yourself in the public eye does not mean you can wow an audience. Public speaking is an art, for some a profession. Like any other art or profession, it takes practice. Being famous or invited to speak does not qualify you as a speaker.

LESSON ONE
Learn as much as you can about your audience so you can tailor your remarks to them and help them improve. What do they want to learn

from you? In this case, was it how to get more coverage, pitch a story, or perhaps build relationships with the media?

Lesson Two

Don't talk about yourself. Share successes, failures, and experience to help others apply lessons to their own lives. For example, I recently heard a speaker talk about her eleven-year-old daughter being diagnosed with cancer a week after her father died. As sad as her story was, she wanted to share her story to help others cope when life happens and the world as they knew it seems to crumble around them.

Lesson Three

Get over yourself. They already like you, which is why they came to hear you. In this case, the speaker told everyone that, if they wanted their story told on "her program," the only decision maker at the network who really mattered was her. Seriously? Arrogance is not becoming on anyone.

At this point, I know you are wondering who I'm talking about. I won't tell you but will offer a clue. I turned on CNN the other day, and she happened to pop up. As I was about to change the channel, the interview caught my attention. It was a meaty conversation, and admirably, she didn't let her subject off the hook. As a former reporter, I was impressed. Then, bam! She blew it. In the middle of an intense conversation about presidential politics, she started talking about herself, her family, and her personal beliefs. Who cares?

Your job as a communicator is to provoke thought and facilitate understanding. There's nothing wrong with sharing your experiences as long as your audience can apply lessons learned to their own lives.

If you simply want people to tell you you're wonderful or you're delivering lines in hopes of applause, you're there for you and not for them. If that's the case, you'll blow it every time and likely have no clue that you did.

Writing For The Eye Is Not Writing For The Ear

I was preparing to work with a researcher who had to give an important thirty-minute talk to investors. I asked her to send over her remarks for me to look at before we got together. I got the e-mail, hit Print, and left my office for a few minutes.

When I return, the printer is still printing. Thinking that something was wrong with my printer or that I'd accidentally told it to print multiple copies, I scrambled through the pages only to realize the endless ink spewing into the print tray was all hers! Fifty pages. Single spaced. Written word for word.

Like many technical people, this person doesn't understand the difference between writing for the eye and writing for the ear. Eyes can read white papers, articles, memos, and e-mails that are often ripe with long sentences and multi-syllable words. Eyes can glance through verbose information, re-read it if something is not initially understood, or put it down and return later.

Ears can't rewind or replay what a speaker has said if they missed something or need clarification. There is nothing wrong with writing out a speech word for word. In fact, it's what you should do. However, if you try to speak it the same way, you will surely lose your audience.

When we talk with people, we don't read to them. Rather, we have conversations. Our sentences are shorter, sometimes spoken in phrases, and we naturally pause between thoughts. Our pitch, tone, and pace automatically vary. You should think of delivering talks and presentations the same way.

When we write for the eye to read, we are more likely to keep our eyes down to find our place instead of making eye contact with our listeners. We also tend to hold on to the podium instead of gesturing or moving as we do when conversing.

After you've written your talk, it's best to go back through it line by line and speak it aloud, as if you were talking to a colleague or friend. Look for places to shorten sentences, eliminate and simplify words, and put thoughts into phrases to help you be more conversational. Often, recording it and playing it back will help you hear how you'll come across to others.

For example, instead of saying, "The production efficiencies will promote versatility and enhance capacity in an economically feasible way," which is how you might write it, when explaining it aloud, you might say, "Being more efficient at our production facility means we can produce and distribute products faster."

Additionally, instead of single-spacing words, double-space them. It's easier to find your place when there is white space between lines. Pump up the fonts as well. We typically write in twelve-point fonts, but larger letters are easier to see when speaking. It's also helpful to type your talk in the center of the page, leaving the top and bottom of the paper blank so your audience isn't seeing the top of your head when you glance down.

Like an animated conversation, people engage as soon as we talk. For example, if we're excited about the Philadelphia Eagles, we might start the conversation by saying, "Did you see that game? The Eagles were awesome!" Then we would talk about the plays and details.

Talks and presentations should also grab attention as soon as you speak. Instead of reading the agenda word for word or spending the first few critical minutes telling people what you are going to talk about, get to it as quickly as possible, as you would in a conversation. Look at the difference:

Unexciting: "So I thought I'd start by talking about the complexity of our system and emphasizing the importance of our strategy to create synergy and develop global programs, which is the theme we want to come through today because we aspire to be a world leader. What I would say is…"

Engaging: "We have made tremendous progress in the past year, and thanks to each one of you, we are well on our way to becoming a global leader. Today, we are excited to announce several new initiatives and international partnerships that will continue to advance our goals."

Studies say listeners decide to tune in or tune out in the first minute of your talk, which is why you need to address what they care about quickly. Using phrases such as "So I thought I'd start with…" or "What I would say is…" eats up your time and theirs.

Instead, you can provide an overview of what you're going to talk about, present a problem that you'll solve, or share a story or experience that drives an important message. You can also state a staggering statistic or ask a thought-provoking question to set the tone and command attention.

Use phrases such as "what this means to you" or "the reason this is important," as you might when conversing with someone face-to-face.

This also helps your listener better understand how the information you're sharing affects or benefits them.

Closing remarks are similar. "Thank you" or "Are there any questions?" is not an effective close. Your final words are your last opportunity to drive home a message or call to action. A few more reminders:

PRACTICE ALOUD
Always practice aloud. This will help you enunciate, eliminate buzzwords, and edit as you go so your talk is easy for the ear to understand.

BULLETPROOF
When you have practiced and know it really well, try to turn the words into bullet points so you can talk, gesture, and sound as if you are having a conversation.

INTERNALIZE, DON'T MEMORIZE
If you try to memorize your speech, you risk not being in the moment because you will be too focused on what you should say next. You don't have to say it the same way every time.

Finally, think of your talk as an extension of yourself. You're an expert speaking to help others better understand what you know. If you are engaging and strive to make sense of information for them, they should be able to listen with their ears even if their eyes are closed.

"Dumb" Is Not A Nice Word

A client of ours has started a new initiative but is struggling to get anyone to sign up. I asked what the initiative is about and was told it's a savings model that benefits members if they meet certain quality and cost metrics. "What do they save?" I asked.

"Well, *they* don't really save anything," I was told, "but they can reduce costs for their customers."

"That sounds good," I said, "but how does it work?"

"Well," they explained, "they go to a website, sign up, and receive a free membership."

"What does the membership get them?" I asked.

The reply was, "What do you mean?"

So I restated the question. "Why would someone want to join?"

Looking annoyed, the key spokesperson said, "Because we'll share a savings model with them, and if they use it correctly, based on performance, we can offer a cost reduction portion measured as a reduction in the total cost expressed as cost per member per month from the baseline year to the contract year."

"That sounds complicated," I said.

Sounding more irritated than before, she informed me that, while it may be confusing to me because I'm not in her business, the people she's reaching out to understand what she's talking about.

"Really?"

"Yes," she insisted. She said that the initiative is about facilitating relationships between her organization and the members they want to attract.

"But how can you facilitate a relationship if they don't understand why they need what you're providing for them?" I asked.

Silence.

"You sent me an e-mail saying no one is signing up. You sent me another e-mail saying you can't close any deals because no one will implement your recommendations. And when we spoke by phone, you said every time you meet with people, they ask a lot of dumb questions. So perhaps the problem," I wondered aloud, "isn't them but could be your approach."

More silence.

What this client and many people who are too close to their information unintentionally do is fail to help listeners understand what's in it for them. How will they benefit if they join? What will they get that they aren't receiving now? If you were them and not you, what would attract you to spend money? If you had to explain this to a smart person who didn't understand your business, what would you say?

You might be a reputable organization, but that doesn't mean people will come running to partner with you. If you want them to opt in, then you need to stand out. You also need to welcome questions regardless of how "dumb" they may sound.

As a former journalist, I learned that there is no such thing as a "dumb" question. If someone asks it, then it's an opportunity for you to further explain, engage, and pique their interest. If you classify my question as "dumb," it might signal you think I'm "stupid" or "ignorant." "Dumb" is not a nice word.

> ## If you classify my question as 'dumb' that might signal you think I'm 'stupid' or 'ignorant'

Too often, because we understand what we're talking about, we assume that other people should understand too. But your job as a communicator is to facilitate understanding. That means speaking as plainly as possible to help your listener understand how the information can benefit or affect them.

If you want to be certain you're getting through, ask a friend or family member who has nothing to do with your business to read what you've written or listen to what you're saying. If they're confused, consider making some adjustments. Here are five ways to help you communicate clearly.

MAKE THEM CARE

Simply saying, "This is a great program, and you need to sign up" doesn't mean anything to your listener. Help them understand what's in it for them. Often, you can do that by immediately addressing the challenge or problem they face. Then you're better poised to help them understand how your program can solve those problems.

Three-Minute Rule
Let's say you have three minutes to brief key decision makers on a complicated issue. How can you tell them what they need to know in three minutes? Pick the two or three most important points they need to hear to help you edit yourself.

Audiences Are Not Created Equal
What seems simple to you might be confusing to someone else, so it's important to assess audience concerns before you start talking. For example, let's say you have to update the boss on the progress of a product launch. Even though he or she might be familiar with the process, do they really need to know everything you know? Your colleagues might be interested in all the details, while the boss is more concerned with costs, time to market, competition, access to partners, and stock price.

Don't Assume They Know What You Know
In the case of the client with the new initiative, they assumed that, because everyone they speak to is concerned about health care costs and the membership is free, everyone would jump on board. What they neglected to do was explain what the new initiative was, how it could help save money, and how a more streamlined, standardized process might improve outcomes.

Talk with Them, Not at Them
Just because you have an opportunity to share information doesn't mean you should keep talking. Pause. Ask and answer questions so the conversation is a dialogue and not a monologue.

Remember, communicators are made, not born. It takes work to get your point across clearly and concisely. After all, what good is putting endless hours into research, cost-saving initiatives, or new programs and products if you can't clearly communicate how they will help the people you hope will benefit.

Be The Person Others Came To See

I was stressing over an upcoming keynote when my husband asked me why I was so worked up about it. "There will be over a thousand people there," I told him.

"So what?" he wondered aloud. "When you were on TV, you used to speak to millions of people, and it never bothered you."

"Well, that's different," I said. "I didn't have to look at them!"

That's when the lightbulb went on. Yes, I make my living teaching people how to become better communicators, and for the most part, I'm a confident speaker. But his remarks sparked a new level of understanding regarding our clients. It's far easier to present to people when you don't have to look them in the eye. And it's far less nerve wracking when people are not staring back at you.

Compared to what our clients must do on platforms and in meetings in the glare of judgmental eyeballs, talking to a television camera is a cinch. Unlike a real audience, the camera doesn't react. It doesn't scowl, text, sleep, or stare back at you in defiance.

Public speaking can rattle even the most seasoned communicator. It's a natural fear and a good fear. *How can this type of terror be good?* you're probably wondering. Because if you aren't nervous, it means you don't care about how you're coming across. Seasoned speakers don't get rid of their fears. They simply learn how to manage those shaky nerves.

Former President William Jefferson Clinton, often referred to as a master communicator, was a terrible public speaker. In fact, he was almost booed off the stage during a rambling 1988 keynote at the Democratic National Convention, where the biggest applause was heard when he said, "In conclusion…" After that, Clinton spent much of his career focusing on becoming the best communicator he could be.

Billionaire businessman Warren Buffet was another terrified communicator. Published articles claim Buffet was so nervous that he would choose college classes where he didn't have to get up and speak in front of people. All that changed when he started his career and discovered he could never reach his full potential if he couldn't clearly communicate his ideas to others.

Then there's former presidential candidate Al Gore. During the 2000 presidential campaign, Gore was awful. I campaigned with him when I ran for the Pennsylvania State House the same year. I remember his stiff arm around my shoulders as we posed for pictures, and when reporters asked for comments, he sounded as if he were trying to recall a memorized script.

It wasn't until he launched the documentary *An Inconvenient Truth* that he connected with the public in a genuine, heartfelt way. Gone were the scripts and pretenses. Passion and personality took center stage.

Too many people fail to equate public speaking with performing. You are "on" anytime you stand in front of a camera or a room. The key is authenticity. People didn't come to see an act or a slide show. They came to hear you.

Back in my television days, viewers always seemed so surprised when the person on camera acted the same off camera. It's the same in the business world. People want to hear from the person they talked to in the hallway or over a cup of coffee, not a rigid version of that person who stands in front of a room reading PowerPoint slides to the audience.

Here are some simple tips to help you become a more natural communicator.

- Think of communicating as having conversation instead of giving a presentation. Conversations are more animated. They allow for pauses, facial expressions, and gestures that occur naturally.
- Tell a story. Create a central theme and then share examples, anecdotes, and personal experiences to make the talk memorable and relevant to your audience. This helps people visualize how information and ideas can benefit or apply to them.
- Opens and closes are key, which is why you should practice them until they simply roll off your tongue. If you get off to a good start, you'll gain momentum. If you close with a strong statement, you won't ramble.
- Internalize, don't memorize, which means practicing aloud. The most natural speakers are the most practiced speakers. They rehearse every aspect of their talks repeatedly until the words sound natural.

Most of us are not born with verbal courage. It's an expertise that's often honed after making mistakes, feeling embarrassed, or learning that your not-so-terrific communication skills are hindering your success. But you owe it to yourself and your listeners to speak up and speak well. When you don't, you may be robbing them of unique insight and experiences that can influence their decisions and affect their lives.

And if you make a mistake or flub a few words, which you will from time to time, it's no big deal. People want the real you. And they'll take comfort knowing they too are in good company!

Five

Sending the Wrong Message

Staying Relevant During Changing Times

My son and I walked into a bowling alley off a beaten path in Bridgeton, New Jersey. It looked nice enough. It was clean and appeared modern, with a lively banner stretched across all the lanes. The alley shoes looked almost new, and the bowling balls were in good condition. From a distance, the lanes looked shiny and well oiled. For bowling snobs like us, who bowl in weekly leagues and have our own gear, this is important.

That's why, as soon as I stepped onto the lanes, I knew something was wrong. Instead of being able to slide up to the foul line on modern nonskid synthetic boards, the shiny wood alley was more like an old-fashioned kitchen floor that had been saturated with wax to give it a nice appearance. Sliding up to the foul line, which is the norm before releasing the ball, could have been dangerous. If your foot sticks, you can take a nasty fall.

So I walked up to the foul line, and like a child first learning how to bowl, I aimed for the center pin and rolled the ball down the alley. Clip clop. Clip clop. Like the hooves of a horse, it noisily bounced and thumped over the wood until it veered off to the left and sought refuge in the gutter.

It's easy to blame the bowler, but in this case, the fault was the shiny wood, which was warped. At closer glance, the boards were splitting apart. While the alleys looked up to date, they were actually a throwback to the late 1930s, when lanes were coated with shellac and bowling balls were made of rubber. Back then, there was little concern for the relationship between the lane surface and the ball.

Over time, like most products, lanes evolved and were made with urethane-based finishes, and today's balls are far more sophisticated. At this little New Jersey alley, the bowling balls were contemporary, but present-day balls do not interact well on out-of-date lanes.

There is a similarity between that bowling alley and companies that update their products but not their messages. Trying to communicate the same messages without attention to how those messages fit into today's lifestyle is no different. Yet that's what we repeatedly observe when conducting message development and communication programs.

Just last week, we facilitated a communications training for a healthcare company that makes homeopathic products. Their old messages are still accurate and succinct and tell an engaging story, but that story is outdated. They've updated product packages and labeling and have embraced today's social media platforms. But when they speak, they use the same examples they've been using for twenty years even though today's audience is far different from the audience of two decades ago.

Today's audience embraces active lifestyles, healthy food choices, and natural treatments for everyday ailments. Helping today's listener understand how natural products can complement conventional treatments and fit their day-to-day regimens should be as natural as the products themselves. Sometimes that's as simple as sharing everyday examples and anecdotes to make the message more relevant.

Like the bowling alley management that updated appearances to lure people in, a business must focus on how to make those people stay. Companies that fail to stay current by not clearly communicating relevant messages can also find themselves striking out.

Yet, day after day, people focus on what they care about instead of concentrating on what the listener cares about. They insist on peppering slides with endless text because it's important to them. They speed up to get it all in when they're running out of time. They use lots of industry acronyms that mean nothing to the listener. Because they are often so focused on their own agenda, they miss obvious cues that signal their listeners have tuned out.

Perhaps there is a big lesson to be learned from a little alley. Other than my son and me, no one else was at the alley, while our home lanes are packed at all hours. Those lanes are constantly updated with the latest technology, so they can adapt to their customers' needs.

> If you want your message to hit the strike zone, make sure it's customer centric and relevant so it doesn't land in the gutter

If you want your message to hit the strike zone, make sure it's customer centric and relevant so it doesn't land in the gutter.

Short Attention Spans Are A Huge Threat To... Where Was I?

I was sweating through my final abdominal crunch when I noticed the cute twentysomething personal trainer trying to whip a middle-aged woman into shape. He was doing a good job, or so I thought. When I looked a little longer, I noticed he wasn't really paying attention to her. Head down and fingers flying across his iPhone, he was texting, chuckling, and occasionally glancing at the woman now struggling to loosen a lever on a machine.

I knew it was none of my business, but I couldn't control myself when I walked up to twentysomething and said, "Excuse me, if I were paying you to pay attention to me, I would have fired you ten minutes ago."

Looking up from the phone, somewhat bewildered, he stared at me and then said, "If you had been here earlier and maybe saw our workout, you would have seen that I was watching her, but I have this cool app on my phone..."

Do you give colleagues and customers your full attention when they speak to you, or are you frequently distracted and time challenged, forcing you to multitask with only half an ear in the conversation? Modern technology is supposed to make communicating more efficient. However, with overloaded in-boxes, text messages begging for instant response, and an overextended global workplace forcing us to schedule calls and virtual meetings at all hours of the day, our concentration and ability to focus on even the simplest task are threatened.

In an article that appeared at Forbes.com, Daniel Anderson, a University of Massachusetts psychology professor, said, "If your attention is being broken constantly, you actually have to mentally reconstruct what you've been thinking." He went on to say that those lost seconds may translate into lost insights.

Perhaps we need to change the way we listen. That means taking verbal and nonverbal cues from people we sometimes can't see or hear. For example, when sending an e-mail, how do we know the recipients interpreted our message correctly? We haven't seen their eyes or heard the inflection in their voice that tells us whether they are optimistic, doubtful, or interested. If several people are copied on the e-mail, one sentence might mean different things to different people.

Several weeks ago, I observed a sales call with a representative helping his company roll out a new product. He was personal, warm, and enthusiastic and did a great job delivering important messages. But he treated the call more like a presentation than a conversation. Instead of encouraging the prospect to talk about her needs so he could help her understand how his product could solve her problems, he barreled through information like a truck on a freeway, intent on its destination. When she interrupted to ask a question or state a concern, he failed to pause, look directly at her, and guide the conversation appropriately. It reminded me of trying to return a tennis ball the same way every time regardless of how it was received. Focused conversations are like tennis. You wait, watch, and look for an opening to score a point.

Years ago, I was sitting in a Lenox, Massachusetts, coffee shop when this total stranger breezed in and plopped down at my table.

"Hi," she said. "Okay if I join you?"

I looked around at all the empty seats but thought better of pointing that out to her.

"Sure," I said. "No problem."

I don't remember her name, and I don't remember much about her, but I do remember our conversation because it's stayed with me all these years.

"You have kids?" she asked.

"Yes, two boys," I replied.

"I have one girl, and I'll tell you something every parent needs to know. If your son walks into a room to talk to you and you're busy, you'd better put down what you're doing and listen when he wants to talk. Make sure he knows that he's more important than anything you have going on."

I'm not sure why that woman chose my table on that morning, but perhaps it is a message we all need to hear. If you want others to respect you, then be present when people speak to you. That means giving them your complete attention. No ifs, ands, or buts.

Striking Out On Leadership Development

The e-mail from an old client came out of the blue. She was excited to reconnect again because she had an opportunity to bring us in to work with some people at her new company. She wanted to set up a phone call with me and her new boss, the head of leadership development. However, to be transparent, she wrote, "The boss might want to go in a different direction because she has no knowledge of you or what your firm brings to the table and has worked with other people like you."

Reading between the lines, it sounded to me as if the boss probably didn't really want to talk to me but was doing her employee a favor. That's okay. I looked at it as an opportunity to get in the door if I could gain a better understanding of the boss's needs and how we could help.

I knew it was the right attitude, so I dialed into the call. Following a brief introduction by the person who recommended us, the boss's first words were, "What is your approach"?

I wasn't sure what she was asking, as our services vary, so I urged her to tell me a little about her needs. Strike one. She didn't think that was necessary and said, "I want you to tell me what my people will learn from you if I send them to your class."

Realizing I needed to act quickly, I ticked off ways we help people communicate more effectively to get results and explained that our programs were highly customized as opposed to cookie-cutter classes. Strike two. I wasn't doing too well.

As the call went on, she told me what we should be teaching and how we should teach it and questioned our techniques. Perhaps I was the one not communicating effectively, so I tried again. This time, I explained our methods, offered examples, and walked her through what a session might look like. She wasn't buying what I was selling. Strike three. I knew we were out.

As I listened to her preach, it was clear she had participated in communications training before and liked her former coach. Aha! That's when the lightbulb went on. I was not the problem. In fact, this had nothing to do with our capabilities. She wanted to work with that individual but had been cajoled into calling me and was annoyed at wasting her valuable time.

So the call ended, but not before she said, "Why don't you send me a brief proposal with costs and references, but don't spend too much time on it?" Ouch. Some people might have said, "Why bother?" Believe me, I thought about it. But you never know what might happen, and I felt I owed it to my former client, who really wanted to work with us. So I put it together and hit Send.

A few minutes later, the phone rang. No, it wasn't the boss but my original client, who began apologizing for the boss. In confidence, she told me the new boss was opinionated and didn't have great communication skills. Then, as I'd guessed, she revealed that the boss wanted to work with someone else but felt pushed into calling me even though she didn't want to.

I'm fairly certain everyone reading this column has had such moments with clients or prospects. But how many of them oversaw leadership development? This woman certainly has the right to work with anyone she likes, but as the head of leadership development, she should be setting an example and earning the respect of every single person on her team. Instead, her employee is now bad-mouthing her to me. If she's criticizing her to an outsider, you can bet she's talking about her on the inside.

Forbes columnist Mike Myatt wrote on leadership, "Show me a leader with poor communication skills, and I'll show you someone who will be short-lived in their position." I have no way of knowing how long this boss will last, but her LinkedIn profile shows she's bounced from company to company like a baseball free agent bounces from team to team.

> ## Being in a position of leadership does not make someone a leader

Being in a position of leadership does not make someone a leader. Those who overcommunicate can be just as harmful as those who don't communicate at all. Both can signal an inability to welcome new ideas and approaches, suggesting that the boss cares more about his or her own opinion than the collective ideas of the team. They may get that team on base from time to time. They may even win a few games. But they will surely lose the championship in the end.

Boarding Planes: A Theater Of The Absurd Version Of Me-First Americans

I fly a lot. On the carrier I fly with most, that means I'm considered preferred, which doesn't get me much other than being called to board the plane before most passengers. However, there are those who have more elite status than I, so they board before me. There are chairman's preferred, who are clearly preferred over me. Airline marshals and members of the US military rightfully board early. So do people who work on the plane.

Then there are people with legitimate disabilities and those who need assistance. They board before me too, as they should. But there is an entirely new group of people who have started to board early. These are the people who claim to need assistance.

Recently, I have observed more and more people standing in this line. Sometimes the line is fifteen to twenty people deep. Only, by my observation, most are walking and, in some cases, running to get in line. No canes. No wheelchairs. No aides or helpers. No visible signs of needing assistance, except for those with so-called therapy dogs.

My guess is they want to get on the plane early before the overhead bins fill up and they're forced to check baggage. I couldn't help but wonder how all these people can move to the front of the line.

So I asked the gate attendant. She said that all you have to do is ask for a pass.

"But don't you have to be visibly impaired?" I asked.

"No," she said.

"What about proof, like a doctor's note?" I asked.

"No to that too," she answered.

"And you don't even have to provide your e-mail or sign up for a credit card or something," I asked.

"No."

So I asked if I could have one of those passes so I could move closer to the front of the line where I'm supposed to be anyway. She said she couldn't give me a pass because I didn't need assistance.

"But," I said, "you just said all I had to do was ask."

Slightly annoyed, she said that, if she let me preboard, she'd have to let others who didn't need assistance preboard too. I pointed out that this was exactly what was happening.

Clearly exasperated with my questions, she asked me to move aside, so I did. I counted seventeen people claiming to need assistance who preboarded the plane before me. That's in addition to all the other preferred-status people I mentioned.

By my calculations, after they all boarded, including the other zone one people in front of me, I was about thirty-second in line. Truthfully, I didn't care if people were in front of me. We'd all get there at the same time, and because I was in zone one, there would still be plenty of room for my bag in the overhead. It was simply a matter of curiosity. I wanted to understand why it is so easy for some people to buck the rules.

So I went on the airline website and searched "preboarding rules." It said that, if you have a mobility disability and would like special seating or need additional time, call at least 24 hours before your scheduled departure. Easy enough. Perhaps that's why so many people were in line.

Then I started to wonder if it was just this airline. So the next time I flew another airline, I went to the gate attendant and asked if I could board early because my back was bothering me. Without even looking at me, she handed me a board-early card, which I then gave to an older woman who seemed to need it more than me.

Clearly, the airlines need a better early boarding system. With threats of terrorism, baggage hassles, delays, overbooked flights, and security breaches, this is likely not a priority.

However, last year, United Airlines took the lead in addressing the issue when they ended preboarding for families traveling with young children. Parents protested. Some even said they wouldn't fly United anymore if they couldn't get their kids settled before everyone else elbowed their way onto the plane and into others as they tried to shove their oversized bags into the shrinking overhead bins.

But the airline didn't give in and instead said they were trying to simplify the process and reduce the number of boarding groups so the rules were fair to everyone. That is what strong leadership should strive for: treating people equally.

Country singer Willie Nelson was once asked what it takes to be a good leader. When I pose that question in my programs, I receive answers such as "authentic," "good communicator," "credible," "confidence," "integrity," and "fairness." All are admirable traits. Nelson has a different take. He said, "Being a good leader is just finding a bunch of people going in the same direction as you are and jumping in front of them!"

This was clearly intended as a joke, and while cutting in line may not seem that big of a deal in the scheme of things, it hints at a bigger problem. Not only is jumping in front of people poor behavior but people who knowingly cut in line at airports probably do the same at the supermarket, in traffic, at restaurants, at the theater, at sporting events, and anywhere else they feel the rules don't apply to them.

So, while Willie Nelson may have been kidding, people who game the system are quite serious. Unfortunately, their disregard for others is no joking matter.

Are You Hiding Your Holiday Candy In The Meat Aisle?

Recently, I went to my local market in search of Hanukkah candy for a holiday party. It wasn't in the candy aisle, so I asked for help.

"Check where we keep the holiday foods," I was told. It wasn't there either. So I asked again.

"It's probably where we keep the ethnic foods." No luck, so I decided to go elsewhere.

As I was heading out the door, a checkout employee yelled after me, "Wait, I found the candy you're looking for. Follow me."

And there they were. Boxes of chocolate Hanukkah gelt (money)—in the middle of the meat aisle.

It makes perfect sense. That is, if you want to send your customers on a scavenger hunt. While customer frustrations likely peak at the holiday season when so many of us are out and about, how easy do you make things for your own customers year-round? Do they struggle to understand how you can help them? Is your website tough to navigate? Do they sometimes need a dictionary to interpret your e-mails?

I received an e-mail from an agency asking us to compete for their business. They said the quote should include a certain acronym that I didn't understand, and the acronym should be accompanied by a "compliant after action report." To make sure we were even qualified to bid, I e-mailed the contact person, explaining that we were communications pros and asked if that was what he was looking for.

His response was more confusing than his initial e-mail. To paraphrase, he said they were looking for a [more acronyms] compliant [another acronym] to build a cohesive cadre. He then explained that he wanted us to assist with [another acronym] through the use of subject matter experts and additional extended staff operations under the direction of [yet another acronym]. At this point, I figured I'd probably understand some of the acronyms if we were indeed qualified and that what they should request from us is guidance on how to communicate clearly.

Regardless of how much your specific audiences know about your business, it's up to you to make sure they understand what you want. That means clear, concise communication. If you send a long-winded e-mail, they may have to read it several times. That takes up their time, which you are inadvertently not respecting. Limit your e-mail to a few points, separated by some white space, that can easily be read on one screen. The same goes for voice mail. Keep it brief.

While most of us don't purposely set out to confuse our listeners, we can mistakenly assume they know more than they know or that they think like us. For example, on line with a computer help desk recently, I asked the technician what he thought the problem was. He replied that the crawler wasn't working. What?

He said, "You know, the web robots." What he meant was that there was something wrong with a program that allows search engines to find you. Now I got it. He was speaking tech talk, but his talk was not my talk.

Speaking the language, as we've heard it phrased, doesn't mean peppering your conversations with workplace jargon or technical terms you think someone should understand. It means telling people what they need to know in words that help them comprehend.

Hiding the Hanukkah candy in the meat aisle is a little bit like tech talk. It might make perfect sense to the stock person who is intimately familiar with the store but never shops there.

The same goes for your company. Most people don't want to wade through oceans of information and choices. They want to know how you will solve their problems and make things easier for them. When we minimize and simplify, the candy is much sweeter to buy.

What Behavior At The Gym Tell Us About Our Co-Workers

I have a theory. I think the way people behave at the gym directly translates to how they conduct themselves at work. Admittedly, I have no proof that the two are related, but I regard myself as an astute observer of gym and workplace behavior since I spend a lot of time in both places.

GYM BEHAVIOR #1

Just today, I patiently waited for someone to finish using an exercise machine at my gym. As she exited and I moved toward the equipment, a man barreled past me and hopped on. I said, "Excuse me; I was waiting for this machine." He looked at me, stuffed his ear buds in his ears, and pretended he didn't hear me. My first inclination was to yell at him, but I knew that would cause an unnecessary scene. So, opting for exercise etiquette, I found another piece of equipment to take my frustration out on.

WHAT IT MEANS AT WORK

At work, this guy is either oblivious or insensitive to his co-workers. According to management professor Robert Preziosi, IQ is not a factor when it comes to people who just don't get it. He says, "People who don't pay attention to cues in the environment continue in a behavior that's not appropriate." He goes on to explain that these people aren't accountable because their inattentiveness prevents them from learning how to act appropriately.

GYM BEHAVIOR #2

Then there are those who speak so loudly on the phone as they huff and puff next to you that they drown out anything you might be listening to, including your own thoughts. If you give them the evil eye or politely ask them to not speak so loud, they act as if you've interrupted them.

What It Means at Work
Aside from being rude and signaling that their time is more important than yours, it also means they don't value being fully present by giving complete attention to people they're speaking with. In meetings, they are probably texting, checking e-mail, and excusing themselves to tend to other business.

Gym Behavior #3
There are few things as gross at the gym as people who leave equipment soaked in sweat without wiping it down. These are the same people who leave dirty towels on the floor, don't put equipment away, and fail to toss used tissues in the trash.

What It Means at Work
It means they are inconsiderate and exhibit slob tendencies. Their desks are likely messy. They are probably the people who borrow things from others and forget to return them. They leave trash on the table in the lunchroom and exit conference rooms without cleaning off the whiteboards.

Gym Behavior #4
It is not uncommon for some people to hog equipment and ignore the time limit sign. When the gym is crowded, this means others can't always complete their workout.

What It Means at Work
People who monopolize gym equipment also hog conference rooms, phones, copy machines, and office supplies. At meetings, hogs tend to

interrupt, dominate conversations, and fail to understand the concept of equal opportunity.

GYM BEHAVIOR #5

Gyms are notorious for fashion. There are the muscle men showing off in tight, sleeveless string tank tops and the flashy, curvy women strutting by in low-cut sports bras with matching accessories. To me, it seems these people enjoy being noticed.

WHAT IT MEANS AT WORK

Like siblings who vie for their parents' attention, grown-ups try to impress the boss, stand out from the crowd, or receive recognition for accomplishments. It's not a bad thing unless they're wearing those string tops and sports bras to the office.

GYM BEHAVIOR #6

There are few things more annoying in gyms than unsolicited advice from those without credentials who think they know it all when it comes to exercise. They want to tell you the right way to stand or lift or how to get rid of cellulite you hadn't noticed before.

WHAT IT MEANS AT WORK

At work, these people want to tell you how to do your job or point out problems you may not realize you had. They constantly offer advice whether you want it or not.

The gym, unlike an office, is a public place. That means you're only stuck with these people and their annoying habits until their workout is over. In the workplace, however, you can't get rid of them that easily, and their annoying behavior can become toxic and affect your morale. If that's happening, when someone continually exhibits aggravating behavior, try telling them what's bothering you, but do it nicely and privately. If the situation grows worse, it may be time to talk to a manger or boss.

Whether at the gym or the office, bad behavior stinks up the place, and there should be no excuse for it.

Six

PROCEED WITH CAUTION

South African Church Scam Artists Pray For Your Faith

The e-mail came from Phil Dooley, lead pastor of the Hillsong Church in Cape Town, South Africa. He was inviting me to be the motivational keynote speaker at the church's international leadership conference to be attended by over a thousand people.

At first, I was skeptical, so I checked it out. The church was indeed real; founded in 1983, it now has branches in Europe, Africa, and the United States that welcome about thirty thousand worshippers weekly.

A Google search on Phil Dooley provided numerous articles praising his work as a former youth pastor who has had an enormous impact on youth and the city of Cape Town. He has over thirty-two thousand followers on Twitter and an active Facebook page with nearly half a million likes. Skepticism quickly turned to flattery, and flattery turned to excitement.

I e-mailed him back for more details and expressed my eagerness to be part of this great event. Curious, I asked how I was selected, and he said that, after checking my credentials, reading articles about my work, and watching my video blog, "we received the Lord's direction to invite you to speak." While I have received valid invitations through the power of the Internet before, to my knowledge, the Lord has never been so directly involved.

After a few more e-mails outlining my fee and requirements, I had both a formal invitation letter and signed contract in my in-box. Excited to share my message on the international stage, I drafted some preliminary ideas, started checking potential flights, and was put in touch with Ed Smart, the event coordinator who would help me with my every need. We discussed audio-visual requirements, potential travel dates, and hotel accommodations, and he requested my bio and photo for event posters.

They were professional and responsive and appeared eager to work with me, as their e-mails were filled with phrases such as "inspiring and motivating our congregation." Everyone who contacted me ended e-mails with words such as "You are blessed," "Have a blessed night," "Remain blessed," and "God bless you." I did indeed feel blessed.

Given I'm a seasoned traveler and have spoken in many countries, I should have sensed the flags.

Flag: Why wasn't this international event publicized on the church website?

Flag: Why were they just hiring a speaker for such an important event only two months away?

Then another e-mail arrived, this one from Linda Jacoline, who said she was with the Department of Home Affairs. She explained that South Africa requires work permits for anyone engaging in work for less than ninety days. Because it can take up to six weeks to get approved, I needed to complete the BI 1738 work permit form and send $875.00, which included homeland fees and taxes. She said I should send the payment via money transfer to the deputy issuing officer in charge of foreign applications, and he would pay the fees directly to the South African government.

Flag: South Africa doesn't require work permits.
Flag: The money was to be wired to a single individual.

Why that didn't sound suspicious is questionable. Perhaps it's because I'm used to visas, work papers, and other forms when traveling abroad. Or perhaps it's because I was caught up in it all. We were going to wire the money in the morning.

If I hadn't coincidentally spoken to my friend Denise that evening, we might have sent the money. When I told her about this opportunity, she said, "Sounds completely squirrely to me." Knowing her good-natured, sometimes cynical humor, I laughed it off until an e-mail arrived a short time later telling me to check out a blog about church scams.

It sounded a little like my South Africa opportunity, but I still didn't make the connection. This scam was in England. It was a different church, and while the e-mails were similar, they were not the same.

So I started Googling, and it didn't take long to find a motivational speaker who said he was taken for more than a thousand dollars. I clicked his link, and there it was. Word for word, I read the exact same e-mail from the exact same people with the exact same e-mail addresses of those who had contacted me.

Not only were they impersonating real people but they were using their e-mail addresses. What can we learn from this?

- Don't shell out a single penny until you've received a deposit or the full amount up front.
- Don't ever give out personal or banking information in an e-mail.
- If someone says a permit or other documentation is required in exchange for doing business, call the embassy and find out for yourself.

I wanted my scammer to know I was on to them, so I e-mailed back, saying, "Nice try. You almost had me, but fortunately I'm on to you." I never heard from them again. I guess the Lord really did intervene on my behalf.

When Inappropriate Comments Threaten The Workplace

When I was climbing the TV news ladder, I had a boss in Milwaukee named Eric, and Eric had a problem that caused a problem for everyone else. He was sexist. What made that even worse is that he didn't know it.

Given this was the 1980s, you might have excused him, as workplaces tended to tolerate a little more than they do today. But, regardless of the decade, I found his behavior completely unacceptable.

As the coanchor of the noon news, my partner John and I shared responsibilities. We helped plan the show, write the show, and deliver the content. We were equals, or so I thought.

Following our broadcast one afternoon, Eric summoned us to his office.

"Who wrote the business report?" he inquired.

"I did," I volunteered.

"Well," he said, "from now on, John will handle it."

"Is there a problem?" I asked.

He answered by saying that the business report wasn't credible when I read it because I'm female. I was stunned into silence, so he continued. He went on to explain that, because John is male, he was far more credible when it comes to business, and people would believe what he said. Then he tried to reassure me that his decision was nothing personal, but viewers prefer hearing business news from men.

Full of fury and disbelief, I told him his logic was absurd and accused him of being a chauvinist. Not one to handle subordinates questioning his pronouncements, he warned me to keep quiet, threatening that, if I didn't, I'd be sorry. Despite John's whispering, "Let it go" and trying to pull me out of the office, I looked my boss in the eye, told him not to threaten me, and said that he was completely out of line. So he suspended me, fortunately with pay.

> I looked my boss in the eye, told him not to threaten me and that he was completely out of line. So he suspended me

In those days, in that newsroom, there was really no one to complain to. While there were women in management, they all answered to men and admitted they didn't want to make waves, as they had their own jobs to consider. But that was a time when only 2 percent of executives were female. Today, while there are still more men in leadership positions than women, we've come a long way since women were primarily portrayed as housewives, and most professionals are more astute about what's inappropriate and what's not. Yet, regardless of gender, some of the same workplace behavior continues today.

Look no further than remarks made by Jenny McCarthy, former co-host of *The View*, ABC's popular daytime talk fest. When debating whether comments by actress Miley Cyrus were anti-Semitic, McCarthy said, "I would always trust any Jew 'cause they know how to make money." When Barbara Walters called her on it, like my old boss, she didn't understand what was wrong with what she said.

Instead of setting an example, McCarthy, like many celebs before her, didn't even bother to apologize for offending people even if it was unintentional. But these unintentional or even seemingly innocuous comments can damage workplace morale if not addressed swiftly and properly by management.

For starters, it's important for management to make sure employees know what is and what is not acceptable. It's equally important that rules and consequences are clear. In general, comments about religion, race, gender, or politics should be off-limits because these remarks are frequently taken out of context or offend when offense was not necessarily intended.

Given that we spend more time at work than anywhere else, we tend to become comfortable with our coworkers and sometimes speak to them as we would speak to a spouse, partner, or confidante. Even when our coworkers become close friends we share our private thoughts with, if they repeat what we said or someone overhears what we say, we could alienate others. A few other guidelines to consider:

JOKES ARE NOT ALWAYS FUNNY
Off-color humor may have its place but not at work. Even if someone is poking fun at himself, someone else could be offended. So ask the person to stop, and if he or she doesn't, report the incident to the boss.

TRYING TO GET A REACTION
Sometimes people say things just to see how you'll react. I once worked with a cameraman who liked to talk about what he and his girlfriend did privately over the weekend. I quickly realized he took pleasure when he saw my discomfort. Once I stopped reacting and simply changed the subject, he stopped. Today, he might be fired or sued.

AGGRESSIVE ACTIONS

It seems obvious that the pushing, shoving, hitting, and biting that typically occur in preschool are not acceptable in any environment. When I was a young employee, an angry boss threw a typewriter through his office window. Everyone looked up and then went back to work.

A national survey conducted by the Workplace Bullying Institute reports that 37 percent of American workers have been bullied at work and that bosses are the majority of the bullies. This includes yelling, threatening, cursing, spreading rumors, touching someone inappropriately, and throwing things. All of them are no-no's.

Finally, managers should set examples for everyone else. It's difficult to enforce rules if they apply to everyone except you. And there's another simple piece of advice that my mother always gave when we were growing up. She said, "If you don't have something nice to say, then don't say anything at all."

A Modern-Day David And Goliath: Don't Underestimate The Power Of One

The four of them sauntered into the conference room. They were big players: the CEO, CFO, vice-president, and chairman of the board. They had a problem and didn't know what to do about it. Their company was sitting on a highly publicized multi-million-dollar project, and they were more qualified than any of their competitors to land the job. In fact, they were the only company uniquely qualified to produce a product wanted and needed by the government.

Yet this was somewhat of a David and Goliath situation, and they were David, not Goliath. That's why their fear was mounting by the minute as time was running out. You see, like the biblical version of David and Goliath, David was just a small shepherd boy who seemed unequipped to take on the giant warrior Goliath.

In this case, Goliath was about to launch a preemptive strike to shut David out of the selection process. Goliath had connections at the top and the political ability to twist a few arms and figure out a way to manufacture the much-wanted product faster and in larger quantities. David was intimidated by the giant and not quite sure how to compete.

So we brainstormed. David wanted to pitch the business by talking about his company's history, formulas for success, and how he could outsmart Goliath. But this was not about Goliath. This was about David, what David could offer, and why he was stronger than Goliath even if appearances suggested the opposite. David needed to concentrate on David by focusing on his strengths, showcasing his brand, and answering a few key questions to think through his strategy in advance.

What sets David apart? How does David help other people? What can David accomplish for this prospective client, and what will it mean to them and their customers?

Once David started to verbalize his vision and how his people have solved countless problems for others, he began to change the way he approached his fears, and his perceived inability to compete started to shrink. In fact, what happened startled David even more than it eventually shocked Goliath. David identified strengths he never knew he had. Instead of talking about his company and his services, he focused on why his approach meant so much to his customers and how his products had changed their lives. He stopped focusing on processes and minutia that only meant something to manufacturers and industry experts and started telling stories about real people, like the customers who valued him.

David became more excited about his business than he had been in years, and it showed. Despite Goliath's best attempts to shut him out, like the little shepherd boy, David put a stone in his sling and flung it. Not only did he get an invite to present his plan but his passion, enthusiasm, and confidence filled the room with a roar that prospects hadn't heard from this little company in years.

Having qualifications, systems, know-how, and experience is not enough. People want to *feel* what it will be like to work with you. They want to *feel* your energy. They want to *feel* your excitement for what they care about.

Undoubtedly, there are many big companies that don't consider small businesses a real threat. Perhaps they should take a lesson from this David and the biblical David. In both cases, David's stone slammed big bully Goliath right in the head and killed him. Both Davids won. The little shepherd boy saved the Israelites. Our David won a multi-million-dollar contract and reenergized his business.

He also won a lot more. Like the biblical David before him, he learned not to cower in the face of adversity. He learned that his vision, when delivered clearly and compassionately, was really what mattered. He learned that, when you approach your fears and work to push past them, you can overcome enormous challenges that will reap bigger rewards than you may have imagined.

A Cautionary Tale About Internet Censorship Abroad

It was about 2:00 a.m. EST when I attempted to log into Facebook from the Shanghai airport. I was returning from leading a crisis communication training program for Chinese hospital executives and wanted to use the downtime to check e-mail and my social media sites. But as soon as I tried to access Facebook, my Internet access was cut off. Then it occurred to me: Facebook is blocked in China. But would they now block my online access too, I wondered, or was I just being paranoid?

It was only a few moments later that paranoia turned real when I boarded the plane. An armed Chinese policewoman called out my name and asked for my passport. This could not be happening. I didn't do anything wrong, did I? They wouldn't really detain me for trying to access Facebook, would they?

After several long minutes of repeatedly looking down at the passport and back up at me, she handed it back and left. Okay, I felt I must have overreacted, so I settled in and forgot about it until a few days later when I tried to log back onto Facebook from home. After numerous tries and hours of technical support, I was told that my PC had been "blocked by a country," otherwise known as Internet censorship, frequently found in countries like China or Pakistan, where governments order ISPs to block sites such as Facebook, Twitter, and YouTube.

I started thinking about the irony of it all. According to published reports, China has the highest number of Internet users in the world but is also among the most restrictive, with more cybercriminals in jail than anywhere else in the world. The government blocks what they don't want you to see. They do it on television and online, reminding us here in America how lucky we are to enjoy freedoms of all kinds.

Yet we have our own versions of blocking what we don't want seen. For example, company administrators who manage page content can take down comments that aren't favorable, and until recently, pharmaceutical brands could ask Facebook to remove unfavorable comments shared with the public.

There are many reasons for content censorship, including undesirable content, protecting children from harm, or controlling access to information for fear of anti-government sentiment leading to revolts such as in the Middle East and North Africa several years ago.

Yet, when we log on, we hardly think about the thousands of websites, articles, and YouTube videos that are blocked and punished in other countries where violations are taken seriously. According to blogger Jaeah Lee, in twenty-three of thirty-seven countries assessed, a blogger or other Internet user was arrested for content posted online. In Vietnam, authorities sentenced four activists to a total of thirty-three years in prison for posting about human rights violations and pro-democracy views on the Internet. So what should we do when traveling to restrictive environments?

Do Your Homework
Know what is permitted in different parts of the world. China, Saudi Arabia, and Iran, for example, monitor and punish unfavorable content. What you post here may not be acceptable there.

Lost in Translation
Individual words do not always translate from one language to another. If you are posting content online, work with a translator to ensure accuracy and context.

RESPECT CULTURAL DIFFERENCES

Be aware of different communication styles, phrases, word choices, and social values. What is polite in one country may be offensive in another.

When you come home, double-check your favorite sites to make sure everything is working. When I finally got Facebook straightened out, I logged onto Twitter but strangely had no access. I called technical support, who told me I had been shut down. Here we go again...

Losing Your Place Without Losing Your Audience

My youngest son didn't speak until he was nearly four and a half years old, which was followed by many years of speech therapy to help him overcome fluency and auditory processing struggles.

So you can imagine our incredible pride when, at 12 years old, he took the stage in a lead role in his camp production of the Greek comedy *Lysistrata*. We were amazed at the number of lines he had to memorize and deliver, which he did with grace and ease.

About three-quarters of the way through the play, which was attended by more than two hundred people at a local theater, he forgot one of his lines. My eyes darted nervously to my husband's when, suddenly, the off-stage prompter loudly yelled out the line to him. The spectators were silent.

For my husband and me, the seconds that followed ticked endlessly. What if he panicked? My stomach felt a little queasy when Alec stopped, smiled, looked out into the audience, and then, pointing off-stage, said, "Whatever she said!"

The crowd roared, and the aspiring actor took an unscripted bow. Ironically, even though *Lysistrata* is a comedy, in this version, Alec got the only real laugh of the night, but they were laughing with him, not at him.

It could have gone much differently. Appearing on stage or at a company event is nerve wracking. Some clients confide that they don't sleep for days before a big presentation. When I shared the story about my son with a client, she said, "I would have just died. I would have been too paralyzed to continue." Yet continue he did, and he received a standing ovation.

What's the worst that can happen if you forget your line or don't remember the next slide you intend to talk about? Will you die? Not likely. Will you be fired? Probably not. Will you make people nervous and uncomfortable? If you act nervous and uncomfortable, others will be nervous and uncomfortable for you.

There was a cougar on the loose in a suburban community when I was a local television reporter, and I was sent to cover it. I stood in the field where the animal was last spotted as the anchor read the lead-in. Meanwhile, the cameraman kept telling me to move back so he could get a wider shot for the broadcast. As I did, the anchor said, "Let's go live to Karen," and I blanked.

I had stepped on what I thought was the largest moving snake in the history of the world. Just in case you're wondering, according to the *Book of Lists*, the fear of snakes ranks number two among most people, second only to the fear of speaking in public. Not only did I completely forget what I wanted to say but I was so freaked out that I rambled for nearly four minutes while the show producer screamed at me through my earpiece to shut up.

Not everyone steps on a snake on live television, but when you blank out in front of an important audience, you feel just as queasy. The adrenaline kicks in, you start to stammer, clear your throat, and say "um" a lot; some people turn a few shades of red. What can you do?

- Stop talking. Take a deep breath, and pause. It will feel like light years to you, but your audience will hardly notice. You can repeat your main point or last point to help you get back on track.

- Rehearse aloud. Broadcasters almost always rehearse aloud to help them quickly recall key points they want to make. In this case, there was no time because we were out looking for the cougar right up to airtime. Thankfully, we didn't find him!
- Use helpful notes. Like slides, your notes should be bullet pointed and easy to see so you can glance at them for recall.

Losing your place, forgetting what you want to say, being interrupted, and fear of failure are more common than you may realize. It feels terribly uncomfortable at the moment, but as my Dad would say, the world will not come to an end.

Staying In The Moment: The Importance Of Being Fully Present

The two women sat on opposite sides of the playground. The first woman was engrossed in an animated phone conversation, occasionally looking up and waving to her toddler when he slid down the slide yelling, "Mommy, look at me!"

The second woman was furiously tapping on her iPhone, unaware that her dog, who had gotten tangled around the sign that read *Please clean up after your dog*, was doing his business right in front of it.

To me, these women were strangers I had passed but noticed on a morning walk. Yet I thought about them as I sat high in the Comcast Center seats at the University of Maryland's business school graduation, where my firstborn son would receive his diploma.

How many times had I done the same thing? Paid more attention to my phone calls or to-do list than my kids running happily around the yard. Focused on my e-mails while my rambunctious shepherd begged for attention.

That lovable dog is now gone. At almost thirteen, she died the morning of my son's graduation. I wish I could have her back. My little boy isn't sliding down slides anymore. He was shaving and driving and entering the workforce that summer. I sometimes long to walk him to the bus stop like I used to do, only this time, I'd savor every moment instead of hurriedly pushing him along so I could get on with my day.

But, as we all know, it doesn't work that way. We lead busy lives and, as the saying goes, often fail to stop and smell the roses.

So I challenge every one of us to do better at work, at home, and at play.

Savor the Moment

Practice being in the moment. Perhaps that's shutting off your phone, computer, television, or radio. Focus on your thoughts or whatever it is you're doing even if it's something as mundane as emptying the dishwasher. Instead of thinking about where you must go or what you should do, just enjoy being fully present.

Embrace the Challenge

View challenges as opportunities. When we see past the hurdles and visualize opportunities, we can change outcomes. Speaking and responding positively when times are tough can give us a greater sense of control and alter the perceptions of others.

Be Aware of Your Responses

Pay attention to your body language, tone, and how you respond to questions or suggestions. Realize that, in addition, to what you are saying, the real message may be conveyed by what your nonverbal language is suggesting. Communication is a two-way street. Create an environment where people feel safe sharing their opinions even if you don't agree.

Be Fully Engaged

We do a lot of work on leadership and executive presence. People always ask, "How can I get it?" While learning to develop presence and hone skills can take time, the best advice I can share is this: if you want to have presence, then be fully present. Give whoever is speaking your full, undivided attention so they feel valued, appreciated, and, most importantly, heard.

As I sat in the stadium with my family waiting to hear my son's name called among 770 business school graduates, I started to zone out. When they hit number 610 and his name had still not been called, I was getting fidgety and impatient.

Then it occurred to me: wasn't this like the woman on the playground halfheartedly paying attention to her child, who will only be a child for a moment? Or perhaps it's like the woman who barely noticed her puppy and didn't stop to realize the dog would be gone in a dozen or so years, perhaps less.

So I looked up and focused. Really focused so I could stay in the moment. And when my boy's name was called, I heard it loud and clear. What a rush! It reminded me of the song the band played at my senior prom by Loggins and Messina called "We May Never Pass This Way Again."

No, we won't. But this time, I was fully present when we did.

Seven

Love and Loyalty

Workplace Lessons From A Venerable Member Of The Family

My dog is twelve. She doesn't have the spring in her step she once had. Like the time she bolted out the garage door and bounded snout first into a freezing winter pond. Her loud, menacing bark no longer terrifies some of the neighbors, who never understood that this sweet, affectionate shepherd is a cuddly oaf who loves everyone and wouldn't harm a fly—well, except for another dog. It pains me to watch our once rambunctious pet limp up the stairs, her hindquarters quivering with arthritis.

When I tell people how she's aged, some ask, "So are you going to put her down?"

Realizing no malice is intended, I swallow what I'm really thinking, which is, "Would you toss aside an aging relative or not provide for a child in need? What about a disabled worker who requires provisions so he or she can continue to do great work for your company?"

I realize our Bonnie is not a person but a dog. But she's our dog, and unless putting her down equals ending her pain and suffering, old age is a blessing, not a curse. At an equivalent of eighty-four people years, her ears still perk up when I walk in the room, her tail wagging in adoration. She's an attentive, nonjudgmental listener when I practice presentations and still assists with housecleaning when she spies a pencil or toy ripe for chewing.

While my neighbors are thankful that some of her bite has left her bark, she remains an attentive watchdog even if she does snarl at FedEx and UPS from the top of the steps, as opposed to flying down them, paws barely touching the carpet in an effort to tear through the front door.

As I look around a workplace packed with four distinct generations of employees and see older workers being put out to pasture, I can't help but wonder if some of the people who suggest we put our dog down harbor the same attitude toward aging workers who aren't as spry as they once were. In places where I once worked, some of the best in the business are being forced out with salary cuts and less desirable hours to make room for more ambitious texting, blogging, and tweeting young professionals who cost less.

Boomers (born between 1946 and 1964) who want to continue working still have much to contribute but should be soaking up fresh new ideas from younger workers, just as these twentysomethings and thirtysomethings should take lessons from the experiences of their sage colleagues. Instead of alienating a millennial (born 1977-1997) by saying that this isn't the way we used to do this, it's important for older workers to embrace change if they want to develop relationships with their younger counterparts. After all, computers have replaced typewriters, and cell phones have replaced pay phones.

Accepting change helps you connect and collaborate with your peers. Similarly, generation X (born from 1965 to the early 1980s) workers, typically labeled as self-starters who want quick results, need to seek opinions and keep communication open with older colleagues to build rapport and make them feel valued instead of outdated.

Like that cherished pet, it's important to appreciate workers of all ages, as an empowered workforce is a productive one. Yes, some employees may take the elevator instead of sprinting up the stairs as they once did, but their view is likely even more valuable than it once was.

I don't know how much longer we'll enjoy our adorable aging pooch, but her unlimited welcome is treasured regardless of where she chooses to sit.

Now Is As Good A Time As Any To Tell People They're Valued

As a kid, I was terrified of the dentist. I would go to any length to cancel or not show for an appointment. At twelve years old, I used to think my parents wouldn't find out, but then the office would call and ask where I was. Another appointment would be scheduled, and the cycle of dental fear would begin again. Psychiatrists would likely say I was traumatized by a dental event. I believe they are right.

My family dentist used to tell me that, if anything hurt while he was drilling and filling, I should hold up my hand, and he would stop immediately. But he never did. I'd be four feet out of the chair wiggling and waving my hands like an acrobat, and Dr. Braunstein would keep on drilling.

As I settled into my current dentist's chair last week, I thought about how far we've come since those huge X-ray machines, gold inlays, and mercury fillings that were the norm. Today, dentistry is far less painful and much more advanced, with digital dental X-rays that can be read on the spot; modern sedation techniques; and natural, mercury-free, colored fillings better suited to match the color of our teeth. Then there's the nitrous oxide, known to some as laughing gas, that they can give you to minimize anxiety so you don't feel the pain of the Novocain injection.

There are days when I actually look forward to going to the dentist. But it helps to like your dentist—which I do. As with a hairdresser, masseuse, or manicurist, people tend to talk to and even confide in those who stay close and keep touching you. I always tell my manicurist that she should hang out a therapist sign, as she probably knows more about what's happening in her customers' lives than most.

Okay, back to my dentist.

Recently, I've had to see her more frequently for some unexpected dental work. That's how I came to learn that her mom was ill. It's been a troubling time for her, and I could relate, as our mothers are around the same age. Like it was a TV show you look forward to week after week to see what will happen next, I looked forward to her mom's continued progress. So, as she stuck her finger in my mouth a few weeks ago, I asked, "How's your mom?"

She was quiet for a moment and then softly said, "She died."

I was stunned, upset, and sad for her. As we talked, she said her mom knew she loved her because she always told her. She went on to say that her mother constantly told her she was the best daughter she could ask for, and she always told her mother she was the best mom anyone could ask for. So, while she was sad, she explained, she said she was also incredibly lucky because nobody can ask for more than that.

If you read my column, then you know I'm lucky too. You may recall that, about a year ago, my mother had open-heart surgery. There were some touch-and-go moments, but she pulled through. Like my dentist's mother, my mom frequently tells me how much she loves me, and I have told her repeatedly how fortunate and proud I am to have her as a mother.

No matter whom you value in your life, now is as good a time as any to tell them. Perhaps it's the employee who needs to hear how much you appreciate his or her efforts. Maybe it's a customer who should be reminded how much you value his or her business. Or a

partner who brings so much to the table but isn't always compliment-
ed. It doesn't have to be a love fest. It just has to be heartfelt.

As simple or trite as this may sound, we all know that we never
know what tomorrow may hold. In those few moments that my dentist and I shared talking, she told me she has no regrets. Do you?

It's never too late to fix them while you still can.

"Hey, Dude, Way To Go!"

When they called out our son's name, we were stunned. To his and our complete surprise, he received our congregation's annual award given to a single person who touches, inspires, and betters others who come in contact with him. We beamed. He beamed. His grandmother cried. Our other son said, "Hey, dude, way to go!" My husband looked at me and said, "We must have done something right."

Perhaps we did, but I try not to take credit. Our kids can be great in spite of us. As a parent, I think it's critical to remind your children how proud you are and encourage them to be the best they can be. Yet, in the workplace, that is not always the case.

Recently, I worked with a newly hired younger client who is clearly poised to climb the ladder. When we were introduced, the first words out of her mouth were, "I can do what you do but don't have the time, which is why they're bringing you in to coach these people." Gee, thanks for the vote of confidence.

In every meeting, she interrupted, tried to coach executives I was hired to help, and continually looked for opportunities to show off to the boss, which meant taking credit for other people's ideas. I wondered, *When she's finally the boss, what kind of boss will she be?*

Leading means letting go. It means taking pride in the strengths of others and utilizing their skills to help people succeed. Perhaps this comes with experience and even age, but an off-the-cuff negative remark signaling your own insecurities and lack of confidence in others can foster an atmosphere of distrust, uncertainty, and hostility.

A few weeks ago, I attended a reunion of former Philadelphia broadcasters. We laughed until our sides hurt reminiscing about days gone by. Yet so many memories focused on shortcomings of past news bosses. There was the news director who threw a type-writer through his office window. His outbursts were so common that no one really paid attention to them. There was the editor who screamed obscenities at people in hopes of motivating them. And there was the person who drove more than one woman to tears when he purposely put her down in front of people. Somehow, much of this was tolerated.

Perhaps it was the era, but leaders and aspiring leaders of all ages can learn significant lessons to help them lead by pushing others to excel.

COMMUNICATE VISION
When you help others understand how they can play a role in achieving your vision, you empower them to contribute and succeed.

SEEK INPUT
Inviting multiple voices and perspectives into the process sparks new ideas, collaboration, and teamwork.

REMIND PEOPLE THEY ARE VALUED
Successful leaders understand that praise, recognition, and emotional sensitivity motivate others to follow your lead.

WALK THE TALK
Clearly articulate your expectations, and observe the rules you put in place for others to create an atmosphere of openness and trust.

As we were leaving the ceremony, one of my son's teachers shared a story about how he made another classmate feel valued. She said they were on an overnight trip, and one of the kids was having a hard time being away from home. She said that our boy nurtured that child until she forgot about being homesick and began participating in the activities. At a young sixteen, he intuitively exhibits strong leadership characteristics.

> ## Good leaders know when to say "Hey dude, way to go!"

Good leaders push others to be the best they can be. Good leaders inspire others to follow. Good leaders lead by example. Good leaders look to others for help and guidance, understanding that it only makes them stronger. Like parents, good leaders focus on others to create an engaging environment. Good leaders know when to say, "Hey, dude, way to go!"

The Message This Holiday: Our Real Gifts Are Each Other

It's that time of year again. December is rolling into January, and as we wrap gifts, race to the post office, and spend time with friends and family, we reflect on much of what happened in the year that's about to close.

For those "A" personality, high-achiever types like me, it's easy to focus on the haves: should have, could have, or would have. The deals that should have come through but didn't. The sales projections we could have made but missed. Or the assignment we would have gladly taken if only someone else hadn't beaten us to it.

For the past two weeks, I have sat by mother's side in and out of hospital emergency rooms and intensive care units in south Florida. She had open-heart surgery, which went well. But just hours after her discharge to a rehabilitation facility, she started sweating and couldn't breathe as her heart began racing out of control and her blood pressure plummeted.

A call to 911 saw paramedics there in moments, hooking her up to intravenous drips as the color drained from her face and portable monitors showed a near flatline while my father and I helplessly squeezed her hand in fear. A medic yelled, "Critical," and like in an episode of *ER*, people in white jackets ran in and wheeled her away to the closest emergency room, which fortunately was across the street. Later, doctors told us she had suffered from severe atrial fibrillation, an abnormal heart rate, and that the paramedics had saved her life.

Instead of fixating on what might have happened or could have happened, I'm trying to close out my year by focusing on what did happen. My mom is not out of danger, but she is here. I spent endless hours with my dad, and while always close to him, I feel a greater connection than ever before. My husband and brothers reminded me of how wonderful they are, and my boys exposed a soft, supportive side that brought tears to my already blurry eyes.

Most of us will face difficult times in our lives. But the whirlwind holiday season that finds so many stressing over shopping, entertaining, and gift giving should prompt us to turn our attention to the real gifts we receive every day. As the year comes to a close, my gift to you is a reminder to focus on the little moments that often hold more meaning than the big ones.

When you get that big promotion, think about all the people and little things they did to help you along the way. When those big bills are tough to pay, as they are for so many right now, try to concentrate on life's little pleasures, like family and good health. It won't pay the bills, but it may provide comfort needed to help you through.

At this time last year, my husband had just lost both of his parents, and my son's best friend had been killed in an inexplicable and devastating accident. It was hard to focus on anything positive, yet through those awful months, my husband kept focusing us back on all the good things the year had brought and how fortunate we were despite what had happened. The haves were also overwhelming. Was there anything else we should have thought about, could have done, or would have said had we known the moment that time would run out?

There is always something more you can say, so say it now. There is always something more you can do, so do it now. There is always something more you can give, and the holiday season is the perfect time to act. People love gifts, so by all means, give them. But when you do, take a moment to remember that our real gifts are each other.

Happy holidays.

Do You Worry About Your Clients?
Three Simple Steps To Keep Your Clients Happy

Sometimes I don't sleep. I think it started when my oldest got his driver's license. My eyes didn't fully shut until I heard his key turn in the lock. Today, that child is in the Czech Republic studying abroad. I have no idea what time he gets in, as I can't hear his key turn across the ocean. Yet I still worry. Knowing his plane was landing at 3:00 a.m. our time when he first arrived, like a sixth sense, my eyes shot open to look at the clock, concerned that he had arrived safely. It wasn't until his text arrived a while later saying all was well that I finally got back to sleep.

For parents and caretakers out there, you understand that this comes with the territory. My son tells me the only person who worries more than me is my mother. And that made me wonder. When our clients have pressing issues, how much sleep do we lose worrying about them? Granted, clients are not children, but if you thought of them the way you think about loved ones, you would probably treat them more like family than just people who help pay your bills.

That means hovering just a little to let them know you care.

CHECK IN, FOLLOW UP
Even if you are not currently involved in a client project, it never hurts to keep tabs on what people are up to. It's easier today than ever before thanks to LinkedIn, Facebook, and the ability to follow people on social channels. Checking in from time to time can mean sharing a helpful article or video instead of trying to sell them something.

RESPECT RELATIONSHIPS
Let's say a former client calls out of the blue to seek your expert advice on something. Give it, and give it for free. A quick conversation that

helps them can reap years of benefits. They'll remember and likely contact you the next time they're ready to hire someone with your expertise. As with family, the gesture says, "I'm looking out for you."

PERSONAL ATTENTION

As your business expands, it's natural to step aside and assign other people to handle to certain client tasks. But don't forget what it was like when you were the go-to person who answered all their calls and went the extra mile to please them. Make sure they know you're still fully attuned to their needs. Without those long-time clients who have relied on you through the growth spurts, you wouldn't have a business.

TELL THEM WHAT THEY NEED TO KNOW, NOT WHAT THEY WANT TO HEAR

While preparing a spokesperson for a challenging media interview a few weeks ago, a communications person stopped me and said, "Please don't ask her those questions, as we prefer she not answer them." Just because you don't want to address tough questions doesn't mean you won't get asked. When readying for any type of communication, it's just as important to prepare for what you don't know or hope they don't ask. Fortunately, her boss stepped in and said, "She's not here to tell us what we want to hear."

Like children, clients need your help. It's why they hire you in the first place. So, if you want them to know you have their backs, be honest and tough, and put their best interests before your own. You'll sleep better, and so will they.

Chance Encounters That Shape Lives

In Mitch Albom's book *The Five People You Meet in Heaven*, he eloquently describes how chance encounters can shape our lives.

In 1981, I had one of those chance encounters with a woman named Lilian Kleiman. She was the assistant news director at WITI TV in Milwaukee, where I had just landed a job as a reporter and anchor.

I was terrified. I had just moved to Wisconsin from a former position as a reporter/anchor in Huntsville, Alabama. I knew no one.

Lil immediately eased the loneliness. She invited me to her home for holidays and included me in all her large and lively family gatherings. During the four years I spent far away from home in an age before cell phones and text messaging, she made me feel a part of her family.

Long after Milwaukee, we stayed in touch—keeping tabs on each other's lives from my marriage and the birth of my children to her continued accomplishments and the unfortunate premature death of her beloved son Danny. We met in Chicago and more recently in Philadelphia. We spoke every year on certain holidays. I adored Lil. She was a surrogate mother to a younger me when my mother was thousands of miles away.

As time passed, we talked less frequently, but I never felt out of touch until last month when I learned of her passing on Facebook. Imagine my shock when I read this post from a former colleague I hadn't spoken to in thirty-five years: "Lil Kleiman passed away on Thursday evening. She was a rare and bright soul. A lovely star. It is not lost on me that she would die on a night when the sky sparked with meteor showers. A mom to us, though not much older than us, she found a way to make each one of us so much better. And then she let us stand in the spotlight and accept the award."

That is the kind of person Lil was, and at work, she managed people the same way. When she nailed an exclusive story because of her great sources, she never gloated. Instead, she stepped away and gave the credit to others around her. When stories won Emmy awards because of her tenacity and talent, she never bragged. She turned the spotlight over to others.

At the young age, by today's standards, of seventy-nine, Lil died from a rare blood cancer. She had suffered for some time but told her doctors that they should spend their time not with her but with people they could help. She said she had a good life, with no regrets. That's the Lil I remember. She always put others first.

Her death prompted me to reach out and reconnect with colleagues I hadn't spoken to in decades. We laughed and reminisced about fun times that seemed like yesterday. We talked about the impact and influence Lil had on all our lives.

Someone I had lost touch with e-mailed, letting me know that, at the funeral, her son noted the role I had played in her life and how she had played a role in mine. Those words touched me in a way I could not have imagined.

Imagine how you might have made an impact on someone's life but never really knew. Imagine that a man recalls what you meant to his mother when he was a child of nine or ten. Imagine discovering that someone you admired and looked up to also admired and looked up to you. Imagine realizing how this person unknowingly shaped who you are today.

Author Mitch Albom wrote, "Heaven can be found in the most unlikely corners." Lil Kleiman could be found in everyone's corner. A little slice of heaven on even the darkest days.

Her passing is sad and unfortunate, but the lessons she shared will live on. A chance encounter can become permanent when we least expect it. We may not recognize the impact this person will have in our lives, but when we look back, we will realize that we are better people for having met.

At the end of the Facebook post telling people of Lil's death, my friend wrote, "And now, the sky is less bright because we lost her."

Fortunately, the radiance of the many lives Lil Kleiman shaped and touched will forever shine brightly.

About the Author

Karen Friedman is an executive communication coach, syndicated columnist, professional speaker and author of the best-selling book 'Shut Up and Say Something' (Praeger Publishing). Today, she heads Karen Friedman Enterprises, Inc. which has been teaching professionals how to become more compelling communicators for more than 20 years.

The firm has provided media, speaker and leadership programs to scores of high-profile organizations around the world. Clients include Johnson & Johnson, DOW Chemical, QVC, Villanova University, Toll Brothers, CSL Behring, Johns Hopkins University, Merck & Co.

and TEVA Pharmaceuticals. The firm also offers executive coaching, strategic consulting and corporate workshops. A specialist in message development, Karen works closely with well-known brands to help them turn words into powerful messages that resonate with key audiences. She is also a keynote speaker.

Karen's expertise was recognized by former First Lady Hillary Rodham Clinton who tapped her to provide media and political training for women in South and Central America. Since then, the firm has conducted numerous global speaker training programs across multiple industries, with a specialty in life sciences and pharmaceuticals. Their work includes coaching executives, key opinion leaders and teaching patient advocates how to share their stories with impact. Karen and her team have prepared scores of spokespeople for FDA meetings, investor presentations, high profile media interviews, IPO's, congressional hearings, employee meetings, panel discussions and industry events.

Before launching her firm, Karen spent more than two decades as an award-winning major market television news reporter whose breaking coverage of local and national events aired on ABC, CBS, NBC, CNN, the Today Show, Good Morning America and Nightline. Her last stop was ABC-TV Action News in Philadelphia.

Today, Karen is adjunct faculty at Smith College's prestigious executive education programs for women where she teaches leadership communications. Her columns for the Philadelphia Business Journal are syndicated nationwide and she hosts *Speaking Of,* on ReachMD. com, a communications program for healthcare professional. She is also the co-creator of Presenters Pal™, the first on line interactive tool to help professionals present like pros.

Frequently quoted by publications such as the *New York Times, Wall Street Journal, USA Today, Forbes*, Fortune and CNN Money, Karen is a professional speaker who has repeatedly received top rated speaker awards. Her articles on leadership and communication techniques are regularly published in business magazines and on-line sites and her popular monthly communication video tips are viewed by thousands of subscribers.

Other published works include "Speaking of Success", which she co-authored with several best-selling writers including the late Stephen R. Covey (Seven Habits of Highly Effective People), Ken Blanchard (One Minute Manager) and Jack Canfield (co – creator of Chicken Soup for the Soul).

Karen earned her degree at the Pennsylvania State University and furthered her studies at the University of Manchester in England. She is a member of numerous organizations including the National Speakers Association, International Association of Business Communicators, Public Relations Society of America, American Society of Training and Development and the Healthcare Businesswomen's Association.

She lives in the Philadelphia area with her husband and two sons. You can sign up for Karen's monthly quick tip videos and other free resources at karenfriedman.com